APPLIED
ANTHROPOLOGY

APPLIED ANTHROPOLOGY

ROGER BASTIDE

Translated by ALICE L. MORTON

CROOM HELM LONDON

FIRST PUBLISHED IN GREAT BRITAIN 1973

© 1971 BY PAYOT, PARIS

© TRANSLATION 1973 BY CROOM HELM LTD

CROOM HELM LTD 2–10 ST JOHNS ROAD LONDON SW11

ISBN 0–85664–040–9

PRINTED AND BOUND IN GREAT BRITAIN
BY W & J MACKAY LIMITED, CHATHAM

Contents

APPLIED
ANTHROPOLOGY

Introduction

The relationship between theory and practice—or at least the conception of it which is usually accepted—has been radically modified in transition from the model presented by Descartes (in the *Discourse on Method*) to that presented by Karl Marx. We must, therefore, begin by situating applied anthropology somewhere between these two antithetical models.

It is clear that theory was preceded by practice, either empirical or magical. As Comte put it, science is born of practical necessities; but though science is born of them, it cannot constitute itself as science except by transcending these necessities and becoming a body of essentially objective knowledge. Limiting ourselves to the social sciences, we see that sociology developed as a result of the European crisis which commenced in 1789. In face of social philosophy's failure to resolve that crisis positivism required the creation of a new science, properly called 'sociology', which would satisfy the two contributory needs which were manifested by the masses—for order and for progress—by discovering the laws of society.

For in the domain of action nothing stable can be built if one does not first comprehend the strict rules of determinism: 'To know is to foresee in order to accomplish.' This famous formula has its inverse: in order to accomplish it is necessary first to know, and it is impossible to know except on condition that—from the first—one liberates oneself from the power obsession. Here we have a first model which is called the 'Cartesian' model because it follows exactly from Descartes' *Discourse:* from theory to its application.

This model is still with us, and we still re-encounter it today in the United States in the realm of anthropology. The remarkable success of the physical sciences has enabled man to control the forces of nature; to a lesser degree, but no less certainly, the progress of biology has permitted the rapid advance of medicine. But on the other hand, we have not yet become able to control social forces even though the 'conquest' of society is more important still than that of inter-planetary space.[1] It is not only more important but indeed more urgent, since 'further new progress in the natural sciences which is not accompanied by the solution of the most important social, emotional and intellectual problems can only introduce more dis-adaptation, incomprehension and social unrest and, consequently, more wars and revolutions'.[2] These are nearly Comte's terms, or at least they express the same concern: how may ordered progress be assured, how may we emerge from the crisis of the twentieth century, if not by constructing an applied anthropology which will be all the more stable if it is based on a truly scientific theoretical anthropology?

Linton shows us that the biological sciences already provide the means for controlling the humidity of the air, the conservation of natural resources and, from these, human health and demographic growth. Political economy, starting from the study of crisis and conflict, has created a barometer to measure the appearance of pathogenic tendencies and thus makes possible the application of preventive remedies. Ethnology, alas, is behind in providing a framework for development for the countries of the Third World. But from every direction we are called upon to catch up.

This first, Cartesian model, is linked to a whole movement in which—whether we like it or not—all the human sciences are involved, and which presses us to rationalise human *praxis* more each day. As early as the nineteenth century, Cournot postulated a law of human evolution according to which humanity passes from 'vitalism' (primitive societies where biological forces are the strongest) to 'history' (intermediate societies where the contingency of events is dominant) and from 'history' to 'rationalism' (which up to the present is dominant in urban societies where Reason dominates the biological and the uncertain). Later, Tönnies saw in the passage from 'communities' to 'societies'—which characterises our epoch of urbanisation and industrialisation—a similar passing from the affective to the rational. But it is Max Weber above all who has spotlighted this movement toward the rationalisation of action: in politics, the substitution of bureaucratic authority structures for charismatic or traditional authority; in law, the movement from customary to rational law; in religion, the triumph of secularisation; and in economics, that of planning.[3]

The anthropologist is caught up in this historical current. In the 'developing' countries, he is called upon more and more to perform a practical task, to substitute planned action for traditional constraints, to make rationalism triumph in continents which, up till now, have had other forms of knowledge—mythical, religious, or purely empirical—and to help 'community' groups of peasants dispersed about the world to become 'societies' by means of urbanisation, rationalisation of the traditional economy, and above all, by programming. But he is called upon to do this within the context of a prevailing model, namely the Cartesian one, that is, to draw his applied anthropology from his scientific anthropology.

We must emphasise this latter point. For this domination of social forces by men, or this control by reason, poses two problems. First, that of determining whether the social world is not different in nature from the physical one. The physical world yields to man's will if he respects its laws. But we observe that, in traditional societies, certain phenomena of resistance to the plans we wish to impose upon them and their rationalisation finally bring about more a disorder than a new order. For man is free and can counter determinism, while nature submits to it.

Still, this is not a fundamental objection; we can readily accept that wherever there are men, and not only natural objects, new phenomena appear. Comte for example recognised this. In the natural sciences, he said, the elements exist before the whole; in human science, the whole is anterior to the parts. This break between the two orders did not keep him from believing in the possibility of transformative action and of control of social forces like that which existed for natural forces. Simply, that action necessitates another strategy, and we know that Comte sought it in education. In any case, to return to our subject, an applied anthropology remains possible if based on anthropological science; it merely will be more complicated than the applied natural sciences.

The second objection is more serious. It is that which concerns the direction that should be given to the control of social forces. Lévy-Bruhl, speaking of morality, emphasised the strength of this objection: 'there is no science of ends, only a science of means.'[4] Surely, many attempts have been made to create a science of ends. Durkheim's is the best known. (For Durkheim, sociology was not worth an hour of effort if it could not be put to use.) It consisted in identifying the end with the normal, and the normal in turn with the functional—and thus, in the final analysis, in removing ethical connotations from the finality of action so as to be able to treat it scientifically.[5] But these attempts to create a science of ends alongside the science of means were all severely criticised,[6] and American anthropologists—so concerned with precisely the elaboration of a scientific applied anthropology—never approach the problem of ends except from the moral perspective.

Yet, is there a universal morality? We may ask ourselves whether actually these ends which we assign to human action in the control of social forces are not those of one culture—our own —which we wish to oppose to those of other cultures. This would mean that planning is in fact nothing but a contemporary form of racism, a cultural racism. And this holds whether or not the plans are requested by the governments of the under-developed countries. For, the analysis of slavery having shown the extent of internalisation of white values by slaves, we may generalise to the internalisation of colonialism by the personalities of those formerly colonised. Decolonisation may well have changed its direction when it was taken in hand by intellectuals and politicians, but nevertheless, the original struggle against the refashioning of indigenous cultures by Western culture, and for the maintenance of an original personality was led by peasants, women and the prophets of messianic movements.

It is this which Berque has defined as the great war between the one and the many—between Western culture adopted by newly-independent countries, and the collective 'personality' or 'identity'.

> 'The world obeys processes of uniformity which weigh not only on the young, independent [nations] but equally on the established countries. The more problems arise, the more they seem adapted to abstract and cosmopolitan techniques, valid for all, and dissociating us from what remains of our identity. By a cruel irony, the very access to history seems to lead to the abolition of the collective subjects who accede to it.'[7]

This phrase recalls that of Cournot of which we have spoken; rationalism abolishes vitalism and the historical. But this rationalism is not a universal value; it is a value of a specific culture—our own. Thus the science of the era of liberalism encounters an obstacle which it cannot overcome—that of ends. Applied anthropology can only supply the social engineer with a set of means. But means toward what, and with what in view? We are thus forced to turn to another model, that provided by Marxism, to see whether it will help us to surmount the paradox which has blocked us from the beginning of this discussion.

* * *

However, before we approach this second model, let us reconstruct the first, as it appears today in the liberal capitalist countries. Just as there is an exact science of biology, and of medicine, which is an applied art, so there is a theoretical anthropology whose only aim is to attain a conceptual knowledge of the real, and a clinical anthropology, which diagnoses particular cases—the state of a social group or a community in crisis—so as to determine for each individual case an applied socio–therapeutic treatment. Practice is thus linked to theory, but they form two distinct fields—that of disinterested scholars and that of technicians or engineers, engaged in action.[8]

Yet, far from submitting to the laws of reality, does not action create reality? Is knowledge, as the scholastics would have it, *adequatio rei et intellectus*, or rather the creation of human will? At the end of the nineteenth century, pragmatism made an initial breach in the Cartesian model, by defining truth in terms of utility. In the natural sciences, facts are revealed by means of our instruments of measurement and our theoretical reference systems, so that they are a mixture of the objective and the subjective. The scholar must manipulate reality to make it speak, and must transform 'things' into 'signs'. This is all the more true in the human sciences. Psychology and sociology bring to light the importance of the law of recurrence: the idea which we have of ourselves transforms us to the point where we end by becoming what we believe ourselves to be. Our concept of social reality suffices to cause us to change it until we are re-creating it when we believe we are only examining it.

It was Marx who created the second model, in its still current form, through beginning unlike Hegel—who believed in the fatality of the mind—with man's dual struggle; his struggle against nature and his involvement in the class struggle. *Praxis* succeeds to *logos*. Ideas are then not simple copies of things, but instead forces which are realised in the world. The truth is that which our revolutionary action verifies. As a result, the old model of applied anthropology—that of the liberal era, amounting to a combination of a theoretical science and an applied art—dissolves; theoretical knowledge develops at the same time as practical knowledge, in and of the same movement of *praxis*. Human intervention in social reality is both action and science at once, since it permits us at the same time to change the world, and in changing, to discover it.

We shall give an example, chosen voluntarily from market theory, a realm studied by non-Marxists, the better to show how profoundly this new model has penetrated our contemporary thinking, though usually unrecognised. In the economics of the liberal era, the market seemed a factual datum which must be described from without (Durkheim said 'as a thing') and explained.

Today, the market has ceased to be a datum and has become a means of information for economists, to be used for the rationalisation of the economy. In doing this, they find that this phenomenon cannot be studied outside a certain political and social context; from *substance*, the market becomes *function*, and this function changes with different social frameworks. Briefly, we have passed from the *homo aeconomicus* of the past to *homo aleator et moderator rerum*.[9]

The sociology of knowledge, as a result of the Marxist model, will develop a conception of science which refuses to separate value judgements from judgements of reality, as the old one did. If man is in the society which he studies, he is both actor and research subject, he is judge and defendant. But we remain bound by the descriptive, and nostalgia for the objective persists, even in this perspective, whether the intellectual is placed above the group, as by Mannheim, or whether, with Max Scheler, we take from the sociology of knowledge more a lesson in vigilance and self-criticism than a new theory of knowledge-action.

Marxist sociology goes further by refusing to define truth ontologically, but rather as a consciousness of a reality which is unfolding through our quasi-demiurgic action. For Lukacs, all thought being by nature linked to action, it is no longer possible, in effect, to speak of a science of society but only of 'class consciousness', making itself understood at the level of the explanation of human facts.

But who does not see that, from here on, applied anthropology can only be formed in a struggle in which it risks being lost while still in the process of formation? We may proceed by following a reflection made by Dufrenne[10] who points out that psychology can readily live with *technique*. First there is a spontaneous knowledge of our interactions with Alter—how we persuade him, learn from him, or oppose him—which then becomes scientific by quite simply transforming this type of naïve and unconscious *technique* into a more considered form of action (educational processes, clinical medical psychology). But in the domain of social science, we are no longer faced simply with Ego and Alter.

We are instead confronted by groups, each of which has its own *technique*. Politics for the administrator is not the same as for those he administers, that of the merchant differs from that of the client. If *logos* is able to unify (and that was the logical and coherent principle of the Cartesian model, which made application or art follow naturally upon theory or science) action, on the other hand, can only divide.

Plurality of groups—this means plurality of ends and of values. Here we are once more, faced with the same obstacle which we encountered above: even if the end is no longer defined by the generalisation of one cultural idea, our own, to humanity at large, it must now escape the group struggle and it will necessarily be based on the victory of one side over the other. Values are an integral part of reality, but as each grouping has its own system of efficacious values, it is now reality which is shattered, forming and reforming ceaselessly in perpetual confrontation, which makes anthropological truth a 'becoming' whose direction cannot be grasped, or a 'prospect' which will always be questioned.

It is none the less along this path that we will persevere; we shall study applied anthropology less as a rational art which is to be added to an objective science, than as a science creating itself in the action of groups and their efforts at modelling and remodelling themselves. Thus, as we see it, it is a science full of value judgements (desires for dominion, hopes for liberation, worries about improvement, searchings for cultural identities . . .), but in this case of contradictory values. Applied anthropology places us in the midst of the struggle. That is why it is the most intriguing aspect of anthropology, though also certainly the most disappointing one for the reader who awaits triumphant tomorrows. He will pardon us if, more often than not, this book leaves him with the taste of blood and ashes.

NOTES

1. Ralph Linton, *The Study of Man*, D. Appleton-Century Co., New York, 1936.
2. Clyde Kluckhohn, *Mirror for Man*, George G. Harrap, London, 1950.
3. A. A. Cournot, *Matérialisme, vitalisme, rationalisme*, Paris, 1875; Ferdinand Tönnies, *Gemeinschaft und Gesellschaft*, 1st ed., Leipzig, 1887; Max Weber, *Wirtschaft und Gesellschaft*, 3 vols., 1st ed., 1922.
4. L. Lévy-Bruhl, *La Morale et la Science des Moeurs*, Alcan, Paris, 1903.
5. E. Durkheim, *Les Règles de la Méthode Sociologique*, Chap. 3, 1st ed., Paris, 1893.
6. In the case of Durkheim, for example, by G. Richard.
7. J. Berque, 'Décolonisation, Intérieur et Nature seconde', *Études de Sociologie Tunisienne*, I, Tunis, 1968, pp. 11–27.
8. Thus, the National Science Foundation distinguishes four sectors: that of applied research in the realm of nature; that of applied research in the human sciences; that of engineers who try to integrate the natural and human sciences (e.g. in the development of a territory); and finally, the educational sector.
9. Here we are summarising G. G. Granger, *Méthode économique*, Presses Universitaires de France, Paris, 1955.
10. M. Dufrenne, *Année Sociologique*, 3e serie, 1948–9.

History of Applied Social Anthropology

1 *The Universalist Mission of Anthropology*

It may be said that from the very first contacts between European and indigenous populations—or at least from the moment when groups rather than individuals confronted each other (groups of traders or of missionaries) a strategy began to be elaborated by the dominant groups, filled with cultural conceit, to change the mentality, transform the behaviour, and reorganise the social structure of the dominated groups, in terms of interests which were external to the latter. It would be incorrect, then, to assume that what the Anglo-Saxons call 'controlled acculturation' and the French, 'planned acculturation' is a recent development. It dates from the very beginnings of inter-ethnic relations.

For the traders, it was a question of creating new needs by means of gifts—giving so as to create new markets for European industrial goods, and by means of the 'swap' (predecessor to the slave trade) to drain off exotic goods toward distant metropolises. For the missionaries, it was a matter of wresting the souls of the natives from the 'shadows' of paganism, to make them receive the Christian faith. One need only read, for example, the *Réductions* of the Jesuits of South America to become aware of this drive for planning—pushed to its extremes. For in order better to change the Amerindian societies, they isolated them, wrenching them from all the influences of their environment and their past, and turning them into a sort of boarding school or college, in which a whole ethnic group was under the control of a handful of pedagogues. The missionaries did not embark without plans, conscious designs, and a developed strategy.

However, we cannot speak of applied social anthropology in that era. First of all, quite justifiably, because at that time a scientific anthropology did not yet exist. The plans developed in Rome, Madrid or Lisbon had to be revised and modified after contact with the realities, that is, with the spontaneous, unforeseeable reactions of the men they wished to evangelise. Throughout this first stage, which may be qualified as pre-scientific, there existed a mixture of reasoning, guess-work and empiricism. The method used thus became one of 'trial and error'. Objectivity emerged by progressive approximations and already the Marxist model turns out to be the one best suited to an understanding of what was happening. For this objectivity was not that of a reality external to the action of the missionary or trader; it was instead a 'construction' of their biased manipulation of men and their groupings.

Scientific anthropology was born only in the second half of the nineteenth century, when the first ethnological school appeared, that of evolutionism. It is not our concern here to show what evolutionism was. Suffice it to say that all peoples pass through the same states of development from 'savagery' to 'barbarism' and from 'barbarism' to 'civilisation'. The only thing we need emphasise is that evolutionism posed both a problem and a duty to the Western conscience. The problem: if all peoples must pass through the same stages of development, how is it that certain among them have stopped along the way or, at least, only advance along the common path with a greater or lesser delay? The duty: if the goal of this evolution—entrance into civilisation—is not everywhere assured, then is not it the role of the whites, who already enjoy the benefits of that civilisation, to help their inferior brothers to achieve it more quickly?[1] And if so, what means should be taken to awaken them and place them on the road to progress? But now, this search for means can go beyond pure empiricism, for there exists a science that explains why and how a population passes from one stage to another. A historicising ethnology lets us understand the lessons of the past, informs us concerning the true processes and paths of our own evolution, which can from then on be applied to the acculturation of peoples still in states of 'barbarism' or 'savagery'. As anthropology becomes a science, by a counter-stroke, applied anthropology is born.

The first question posed by Comte, for example, was to discover whether in this climb towards progress, it was certain that all
peoples must pass through the same stages or whether certain
stages could be skipped. Must they, before arriving at the positive
state, begin first by going from fetishism to polytheism, and then
to monotheism, and thus encourage the formation of Christian
Missions? Or, on the contrary, could they directly bridge the abyss
which separated fetishism from positivism, without having to pass
through the intermediate stages, as our civilisation had done? We
know that Comte held the latter view, and that the Positivist
Church of Brazil attacked Mission activities among the Indians—
whether Catholic or Protestant—accusing them of retarding their
ascension toward progress and stopping them in their spontaneous
march.

The second question concerned the discovery of the cause of
certain halts, or a certain slowness characteristic of those populations that were termed 'backward' relative to our own. Some, following Morel's point of view in his *Treatise on Degeneracy*, sought
physical causes: climate (civilisation is the fruit of a temperate
climate); ecology (unhealthy regions destroy the peoples' physical
health, thus making them unfit for civilisation).[2]

Others, like Allier, in his *Psychology of Conversation among
Uncivilised Peoples*, or his book on magic, sought spiritual causes:
civilisation is only made possible by the control of the superior
functions (reasons and will) over the inferior functions (instinct
and rampant emotionality). Man in the course of his evolution
finds himself, at a given moment, at a crossroads: certain peoples,
those reached by Christianity, have chosen effort; others have
chosen frenzied eroticism combined with paganism. The cultivation of sensuality would thus be responsible for halts in development, weakening of the creative will, and descent into magic
which is, in its essence, counter-progressive.[3]

From there on, applied anthropology varied according to
whether so-called scientific anthropology stressed physical or
moral causes. In the first type of case, the external environment
must first be made healthy and the doctor takes pride of place. In

the second, men must first be changed; society and its culture will change as a result. The missionary, who liberates individuals from their carnal passions, or the educator, who teaches the paths of reason, then takes precedence. Applied anthropology hesitated between these two concepts, but in either case, its own approach is no longer empirical but rational. Here, as opposed to the pre-scientific period, it is the Cartesian model, dear to liberal capitalist economy, that is retained. One begins by seeking the true causes of phenomena in order to be able to act upon them; the laws of nature—social as well as physical—must be respected if one wishes to succeed. It is no longer *homo aleator* but *homo sapiens* who dictates the rules of the only really effective action, since they rest not on the contingency of action itself but on the certainties of science.

But the failure of this first applied anthropology disillusioned those who had promoted it. Conversion was most often only superficial and Christian concepts were reinterpreted in terms of traditional beliefs. Schools failed to change people profoundly; society took back its children at the end of class to undo the white masters' teaching. The 'man of progress', civilisation's delegate to the 'barbarians' or 'savages', had believed that it sufficed to acquaint them with the values he believed superior to arouse the enthusiasm and fervour of their masses. But he quickly recognised his power-lessness, spoke of 'inveterate laziness', and 'congenital inferiority' or of 'diabolical powers' unleashed against the word of God . . . True, an 'elite' was formed everywhere which believed in Western values and assimilated them, but this elite ungratefully then turned against its teachers.

11 *The Problem of Cultural Relativism*

We may take the work of Lévy-Bruhl as evidence of this failure. Emphasising the result of the contradistinction between pre-logical and logical mentality, he saw conversion from one to the other, if not as impossible, at least as especially difficult. Scholars of the period were not taken in, and if the reaction of some anthropologists was so impassioned, it was precisely because they saw in Lévy-Bruhl's work a condemnation either of the missionary

endeavour (Allier) or of the colonialists' work of assimilative
education. In the United States, Boas, who had denounced
evolutionism, just as vigorously denounced as false the idea of a pre-
logical mentality. But with Boas, we come to a second stage of the
history of anthropology, that of the triumph of cultural anthropology, to which we must turn for a moment.

Certainly reason is one and the same among all men, regardless of their skin colour, or the texture of their hair. But it reveals
itself through different sorts of cultural endeavour. We are not to
judge the value of these varieties; there are no superior or inferior
cultures. There are only *different* cultures. Evolutionism's chief
mistake was to judge other civilisations by reference to our own,
and thus to fall into the sin of ethnocentrism. Undoubtedly the
Australian aborigines when they were discovered may well have
still been in the Stone Age, but they offered the observer a social
wealth and complexity superior to our own. Obviously, Eastern
civilisations did not reach as high a level of technological development as did those of the West, but they did, on the other hand,
reach a higher level of spiritual development and metaphysical
knowledge than ours.

Is not the conclusion that emerges from this cultural relativism
then that each people should remain autonomous? The term 'genocide' was not fashionable at the time. But could not all policies of
forced acculturation, assimilation and change of native mentality
or values be seen as a veritable 'cultural genocide'?[4]

The Native Reorganisation Act provides an illustration of this
change of perspective. It was based on the working notion that
man lives only in and by a group, and that each group has its own
autonomous civilisation. Each indigenous community is thus
endowed with a culture of its own, which is historically formed as
a result of the actual interaction between the evolving human
group and the external milieu which enables the needs of the
group to be satisfied. Certainly, Amerindian societies could be
integrated politically and economically into the larger North
American society. But, nonetheless, culturally they must retain a
complete independence in relation to white culture.

Economic cooperation between white and Indian could not bear fruit except through respect on the part of the whites for the religion, customs and values of their Indian partners. Nevertheless, the idea of the superiority of Western civilisation haunted the consciousness of the promoters of this Act, though it was no longer in terms of an *a priori* desire for assimilation. The initiative must come from the Indians themselves, not from outside. The thinking underlying this piece of legislation was that, once the whites controlled the budget and distributed it themselves among individuals or groups, failure—that is, resistance on the part of the administered—was patent. But if, conversely, the distribution of credit was left to the communities, would not a reversal occur? These communities, finally free, would not fail to make good use of it, which implies that they would use it towards the end of Westernisation or acculturation.[5]

It is precisely because the relativism of cultural anthropology is never pursued to its logical extreme, because it retains within itself that ethnocentrism which it decries elsewhere (though at a more theoretical than practical level) that we may speak of the dilemma of cultural anthropology. One of the most famous works of this school, that of Herskovits, which is entirely based on the notion of relativism, ends, paradoxically, with a chapter on applied anthropology.[6] The reader senses an internal contradiction between the beginning and the end of the work; many professors of anthropology have acknowledged this. The word 'contradiction' may perhaps be too strong for, between the analysis of cultures and the final chapter, there is a whole group of intermediate chapters devoted to the dynamics of culture, which is to say, their evolution.

Civilisations do not remain static; they change over time, either by innovation internal to their development or by borrowing from neighbouring civilisations. It should not be forgotten that cultural anthropology was born, with Boas, under the sign of diffusionism, of the recognition of exchange between societies in contact, and that it has always given an important place in its approach—as with Herskovits, Linton and Redfield—to the facts of acculturation, that is, to the process of diffusion as it occurs. Ethnographers' observations show that if men resist change, they also accept from other cultures techniques, institutions and practices which seem good to them. An applied anthropology is then possible, based on these facts of acculturation and on this recognition that the native does accept something from the white after all.

But if we cannot speak of a true contradiction between cultural relativism and the existence of an applied anthropology, we can still speak of a certain discomfort and vague disquiet on the reader's part. And these are not groundless. The history of native action, with its toing and froing, its hesitations and detours, demonstrates their validity. For the era when cultural relativism triumphed ended in similar failure to the era of forced assimilation and of evangelism out of which it had grown. It had been hoped that respect for Indian cultures would finally be actualised in the abandoning of 'the white man's burden'. But relativism merely hid the old ethnocentrism—ineffectively because it arose in a situation of the integration of one world within another. So, far from changing, the native hardened his resistance and profited from the administration's liberalism to return more systematically to his old traditions.

American attitudes toward the Indian reservations were thus to change once more, for two reasons. Firstly, for an economic reason —the increasing value of natural resources belonging to the Amerindians (forests, minerals, grazing land). If the Indians could be Westernised, accepting the Western profit-motive mentality, they would pass from collective ownership to individual ownership. To satisfy the new demands created by the consumer society, these individual owners would be tempted to sell their resources which would slowly become the booty of the whites. To this economic motive was added another, an ideological one, which was actually a reflection of these material interests in the minds of the whites; evolutionism re-emerged. Since evolutionism was still poorly regarded by American scholars, they were to disguise it, giving it a new form and vocabulary. And this became the theory of purely

economic and social development which postulates—like the condemned evolutionism—that Western values are superior to all
others, and that change must be in their direction.

To summarise, during these two great phases of cultural anthropology—that devoted to the relativity of values as against the
ethnocentrism of the first anthropologists, which was meant to
give rise to a liberalism vis-à-vis inter-ethnic contacts; and that
devoted to the facts of acculturation, which resulted in the formation of an applied anthropology and thus, behind the scenes, to a
return to ethnocentrism—this contradiction was finally resolved
by the triumph of the second perspective over the first.

III Functionalism and Applied Anthropology[7]

Malinowski is frank. He shows clearly the significance of colonialism for the origins of an applied anthropology which attempts to
be scientific theoretical anthropology. For according to Malinowski, science is more and more necessary to colonial administrators
if they wish to succeed in changing the societies whose managers
they have become. Thus, all his efforts upon his return to England
were directed toward training future administrators in ethnographic methods, and sensitising ethnologists to the practical and
not merely the theoretical value of their discipline. This is why we
find him fighting against evolutionism as well as the historical
ethnology of Graebner and the Vienna School.

For him, anthropology must no longer throw itself into the
search for a hypothetical past. Instead it must take as its main task
the reconstruction of what the indigenous society must have been
like before the coming of the whites. Instead of reconstructing
history, it must take up present-day reality. Malinowski has often
been criticised, especially of late, for disdaining history. But here
we see the basic reason for it—that a knowledge of the past is
gratuitous and useless. The administrator works in the midst of
men, in the present, and with a future in view. He thus need know
only the real society in which he acts. Cultural anthropology here
yields to social anthropology, which is functionalist. That is, ignor-
ing questions of causality (explanation by antecedents) it will be

occupied solely with questions of function (explanation of present-day social institutions in terms of the needs of the men who have created them).

Thus, it must be shown that the scientific revolution brought about by Malinowski's work and which affected the contemporary evolution of anthropology so profoundly, did not grow merely out of a personal taste, or a sense of the failure of previous schools, or the recognition that all historical reconstructions of the human past had failed and were closer to fiction than to science. In the final analysis, the progress of ethnology from history to psychology—characteristic of anthropology in the second decade of the twentieth century, especially for Malinowski the psychology of natural needs before this psychology became complicated by its more or less Freudian offspring—is a response to the logic of colonisation. If, as Comte affirmed, the necessities of the practical are the source of science, it may further be said that they are also the source of all scientific transformations, such as the major metamorphoses of great explanatory theories.

Yet it is interesting to note that this transformation was the work of British anthropologists and not of French. And this is precisely because British colonisation followed different routes than did French 'civilisation'—it used indirect rule by means of indigenous chiefs as opposed to direct rule by the metropolitan country. The Third Republic took account of the philosophy of the *Lumières*, which had already supplied the ideology for the Revolution of 1789. The nineteenth- and twentieth-century colonialists went to war, like the soldiers of the Year II against the *Tyrans*. ('obscurantism' of tradition proved in both cases to be the common enemy of the republican armies which sought the triumph of Cartesian reason at bayonet point.)

But such a system seemed completely useless to Malinowski, for a new order could not be miraculously wrested from the old; Africans could not be transformed, by enchantment, into civilised men. For our French anthropologists, this was more a magical than a scientific concept of colonisation. In reality, all social change is slow, and demands a good deal of caution from one who wishes to turn it in a given direction. Indirect rule is the only way to develop the economic life and rational administration of a country —by having the natives themselves take charge of changes in morality, justice, education, religion and art, since they will know how to transform them along their own cultural lines, and thus without betraying themselves.

Applied anthropology as a scientific discipline could not emerge in a country which, like France, believed in the simple spread of reason. It could only come to life in a pragmatic country like England, concerned with the facts, taking resistances into account, and always acting cautiously. In any case, the conclusion which emerges from this second system of action (indirect rule) is that one must first comprehend the culture of a people before trying to modify it. Briefly, applied anthropology follows only upon ethnographic exploration. Malinowski did not doubt that this marriage of a knowledge of the facts and of action would be equally favourable for ethnology and for colonisation.

For the old ethnology always wandered along the same paths—myths, rites, peculiar customs; it ended in pure spectacularism or exoticism. But exoticism is not daily life. The anthropologist's practical action, far from jeopardising science, on the contrary favoured its progress, by opening new approaches. Malinowski gives several examples of this. He emphasises the fact that, during the period of which he was writing, few studies had been devoted to traditional political systems. Since change must be made by means of traditional chiefs, indirect rule demands that African systems of power be understood as a preliminary. Too many studies, on the other hand, he says, were concerned with the reconstruction of indigenous civilisations as they must have been before colonisation; but European influence had already been at work for too many centuries for such reconstructions not to be both false and overly abstract. Reality is the dialectic interplay which can be taken up between different civilisations. An ethnology of cultural dynamics, the effects of contact and the phenomena of diffusion must be substituted for an historical one which freezes an often-imaginary moment of the lived present. It may then be seen that applied anthropology does not limit itself to an art in the service of colonisers, even if, for Malinowski, it arises from the needs of colonisation; it attempts also to be science, or at least to renew, deepen and enrich science.

But functionalism was Malinowski's greatest discovery, which caused his name to be given to the school of social anthropology which he created. Let us see how, by means of the facts of colonisation, he arrived at this new conception of anthropology.

What most preoccupied colonial administrators were problems of labour, and of economic productivity. Now labour is a pre-planned form of systematic behaviour, standardised by tradition, and devoted to the satisfaction of the needs of one who submits to it. These needs are, firstly, natural needs (satisfaction of hunger and the fight against the elements). But they are taken up by culture and, having become cultural, it is necessary—if one wishes to see how and to what extent the productivity of this labour may be increased—first to discover the value systems intrinsic to a given culture, so as to be able then to discern how action may be stimulated.

By ascribing the discovery of functionalism to Malinowski, we are not underestimating the originality of Durkheim and, before him, of the organicists. On the contrary, on this particular point we find Durkheim's thought superior to that of Malinowski, and this is why Radcliffe-Brown had to return to it. But that was a question of sociological functionalism—purely theoretical and incapable of generating action. What Malinowski discovered was psychological functionalism, based ultimately on the biological nature of human needs which, consequently, made their manipulation possible—the very object of applied anthropology.

Social institutions are cultural responses to needs, the means through which they satisfy themselves, in a particular form of civilisation. Thus, we cannot casually destroy these traditional institutions so as to replace them with new ones 'made in Europe'. Or, more exactly, each time we destroy an institution in our role as managers of the economic life of a country, we must first find out to which function it corresponds—to which needs and which values—so as to create in its place a new institution which we think superior, but which will fulfil the same function, satisfy the same needs, and which will not seem to be in too obvious opposition to the values which underlie the old one.

The building of a new water supply system in an African village, seen from this perspective, provides a good example of the mistakes which can be made through good intentions which are not based on a preliminary understanding of the 'functions' to be respected. Planners were greatly upset by the physical effort expended by women who had to go several kilometres to get water from the spring and carry it back on their heads to their houses, and by the time lost in this chore. They only thought emotionally about it. But once water was piped into the houses, a sadness fell over the village, and people suffered from outbreaks of depression. This was because the chore of water-carrying had had another, *latent* function—it had given women a chance to get together, gossip together, to complain about their neighbours, and circulate news and decisions.

Now each woman found herself alone in front of the tap. In order to keep the resultant spiritual deterioration from becoming intensified, a further new institution had to be created—fulfilling the old need which was no longer being satisfied, that of amicable relaxation, gossip and interaction. A women's club was formed, which, while satisfying these old needs could also create new cultural and political ones. There could not be a better example, and it has quickly become a classic, showing the relevance of functionalist thought for the establishment of applied anthropology.

iv *After the Second World War*

Britain used her colonies like a laboratory; the United States did not have any colonies. And we have seen how the dominant doctrine in the latter country—that of cultural relativism—should, logically, have precluded practical preoccupations to the benefit of theoretical ones. The path that led here to the transformation of anthropology into applied anthropology did not stem from colonisation, but rather from internal problems of the United States—those already noted concerning Indian reservations which only interested a few and those posed by riots, violent strikes, the emergence of criminal gangs, etc. In a word, the path here is that leading from social pathology to applied anthropology.

Is it not immediately obvious that things will seem fairly different in these two countries? British applied anthropology foresaw its unfolding as preceding that of colonial administration, whose most effective line of action it was its task to dictate. American diagnostic anthropology, on the other hand, followed on the outbreak of crises which had profoundly shaken a community, searching for the causes which provoked them and proposing the most adequate remedies to ensure that they did not continue or recur. To use Kluckhohn's expression, the American anthropologist appeared as a 'trouble shooter', only called upon when the blacks had been massacred by the whites, or when an aggressive cult, such as the messianic Ghost Dance, created immediate problems which urgently required resolution. But World War II radically altered this state of affairs.

Increasingly, as this war was prolonged and intensified, anthropologists were called upon by the government, and their competence was requisitioned to 'neutralise' emotional problems in the armed forces and among civilians, on both the national and international fronts. In the war industries, the whites who had gone off to fight were replaced by blacks; race relations had to be regulated so as to avoid tensions which would have decreased production. Enormous external demands necessitated rationing, but the nutritional level had to be maintained. As a result, biological knowledge had to be adapted to the practical problems of rationing.

In another sphere, foreign propaganda required analysis so as to be countered, and special services had to be created to wage effective psychological warfare—and this behind the very German lines—as well as to strengthen morale at home during a long and costly struggle. In brief, the role of anthropology was extended to new fields, and its character altered, since it was no longer sufficient to diagnose and react, as before; now it was necessary to foresee and to plan. The Second World War thus made possible a convergence of British and American applied anthropology, removing the latter from pure pathology by giving it prospective tasks.[8]

Certainly, as we have seen was the case with Malinowski, this broadening or deepening of applied anthropology was useful for the broadening of anthropology generally. There is always a reciprocal action and reaction of theory on practice, and practice on theory. We may say, broadly, that the gains made by theory as a result of the war were in two areas—that of multi-disciplinary research—since the anthropologists had to work with sociologists and psychologists—and that of the generalisation of anthropology from the concern with simple societies, characteristic of the old ethnology, to complex societies, and specifically our own. These two results of the government's appeal to anthropologists for participation in the war effort—multi-disciplinarity and the development of an anthropology of complex societies—have now become definitive acquisitions of the science of man.

However, as Kluckhohn properly emphasises, all the efforts undertaken by anthropologists during this period were not uniformly successful, and they raised differences of opinion. Thus, after the American invasion of Italy, anthropological instruction was given to officers on the problems of inter-ethnic relations. Politicians looked askance on this initiative, fearing that too close an association between Americans and Italians might precipitate the development of fascist sympathies among the former. The anthropologists replied that contact does not imply complete emotional acceptance, but an occasion for obtaining understanding and information.

Another divergence appeared à propos Japan, at the level of propaganda as well as that of the rehabilitation of prisoners. Anthropologists started with the axiom of human identity, which led them to conclude that all men must respond in the same way to the same situation regardless of their country of origin. But they had to admit that the behaviour of the Japanese, both before and after capture, remained radically different from that of Americans.

The latter retained the same moral code in all situations, while the Japanese changed theirs. The idea of a 'situational morality' was thus adopted by public opinion.

The Second World War demonstrated, then, that anthropology was necessary for concerted action but that, from another angle, it still lacked maturity, both as science and as applied science. Thereafter, the main effort was to make it progress. This effort was further increased due to the fact that the United States became one of the two greatest world powers, and became aware of its responsibilities toward the other peoples of the world and that, henceforth, it would have to act on a planetary basis.

Latin America, India, Africa, the under-developed countries of the Mediterranean appealed not only for capital but also for American experts, to get started on the road to progress. To avoid tensions, factors which might lead to new wars, it was necessary to integrate non-industrial peoples into the world economic community. It was also necessary—for this was another possible source of war—to recognise cultural variety and replace ignorance or misconceptions of this variety with an apprenticeship in tolerance and mutual respect. Anthropology left its ivory tower to enter the schools and life.

We come thus to the threshold of the contemporary period. But before exploring it, two points must still be made. The first is that, if throughout its historical evolution applied anthropology has continuously enlarged its scope—in the end passing from the study of colonial societies to that of complex ones—its basic nature has not changed. Structurally, it retains as its base a model of *asymmetrical* relations. That is, it is based on a stratified notion of societies, or, if you prefer, on the existence of majority and minority groups, higher and lower strata, in a relationship of dominance and subordination.[9] There are groups that are only givers and those that are only takers—'civilised' and 'savage' in the pre-colonial era; then colonisers and colonised, then, finally, the peoples of the Third World if we keep to the inter-ethnic sphere.

If we proceed to the intra-ethnic sphere, following the same model, we have urban and rural areas, whites and coloured people for multi-racial societies, bourgeois and proletarians. As we shall see, contrary to the laws of free acculturation, applied anthropology is dominated by a desire for the assimilation of the minorities by the majorities, who hold the keys of power, and the direction of strategy.

The second point we must make is that the problem which we raised in the introduction has still not been resolved: art or science? And if we wish to give applied anthropology scientific status, the science of what—merely of means, or of ends? We will devote the next two chapters to means and to ends, starting with the one on ends, since it keeps us in the realm of American anthropology, where we must remain for a moment before turning to Russian thought.

NOTES

1. Here we are explicating the facts as they emerge in the 'consciousness' of Western thought of the period. It is clear that a more profound research would lead us to pose the question whether evolutionism—far from being the cause, is not the effect—and whether this theory is not a 'rationalisation' or 'justification' after the fact, of colonisation.
2. R. Morel, *Traité des Dégénérescences*, Paris, 1957.
3. R. Allier, *Le Non-civilisé et Nous*, Paris, 1928, and *Magie et Religion*, Paris, 1935.
4. Certainly, here as above, we remain with the conscious expression of anthropologists. In another way, we could ask in what measure this ideology is like a weapon against European colonialism, to substitute one domination for another. It is curious to note that after decolonisation, one finds American anthropology returning to evolutionism, with White, while the Soviet countries have always remained true to Morgan, who justifies their cultural and political expansionism.
5. J. McNickle, 'The Indians of the United States', *Amer. Indigena*, XVIII, 2, 1958.

6. M. J. Herskovits, *Man and his Works*, Alfred Knopf, New York, 1948.
7. B. Malinowski, 'Practical Anthropology', *Africa*, 2, 1929.
8. Clyde Kluckhohn, op. cit., Chap. VII.
9. This point was clearly seen by Herskovits, op. cit., Chap. XX.

The Dialogue Between the Anthropologist and the Administrator

When the anthropologist works at home, the problem of ends poses itself for him less acutely. For even if he works in a society in crisis, on the integration and conflict of groups, each having a specific sub-culture, it is still true that these groups form parts of the same global society, and these sub-cultures of the same national culture. It is therefore possible to assume that all the people in question share the same values or that they have very similar values. But even so, the problem of ends still presents itself since the anthropologist does not work on his own behalf, doing gratuitous research. He has been drafted, given a job to do in well-defined temporal and budgetary conditions. The time allotted him may be too short, or the budget too small for the results he achieves to be considered sufficiently valid and useful in the long term. In this case, there will at least be a conflict between the scholar's ethics and the decisions of those who have employed him.

More obviously, this will be true when we proceed from internal problems to those which involve relations between several different, equally independent nations. In that case, the problem of ends is generally spirited away or, more exactly, it is not discussed; the goals to be achieved are given *a priori*. In general, three types of ends may be isolated: moral ends, hedonistic ends, and utilitarian ends. 'Moral' ends are especially specified when the use of machines or techniques is involved, which may, like atomic fission, serve for bad as well as for good or further techniques of propaganda or publicity which alienate man more than they serve his needs.

'Hedonistic' ends are involved when science serves happiness or welfare. But it is impossible, despite Bentham's arithmetic, to give an objective definition of happiness; each has his own conception

27

of it. Primitive societies give individuals more security than do the progressive techniques we offer them; change causes more traumas in them than satisfaction. And even if, unconsciously, the primitive is mistaken as to what for him is actually happiness, have we the right to impose it on him by force? 'Utilitarian' ends are those which seem to predominate, linked with economic planning and the search for greater productivity. In general, they are not justified. However, when we seek to justify them, this is naturally not done in terms of the interest of the 'donor' country, but of that of the 'recipient' country or—beyond all these frontiers—of the 'common welfare' of humanity.

F. Perroux is thinking of the 'recipient' country when he defines economic development as 'the combination of mental and social changes of the population which enables it to increase, cumulatively and enduringly, its real gross national product' and progress —taking account of all that these mental and social changes bring with them in the way of unfortunate sequels and wounds (delinquency, prostitution, formation of antagonistic classes, increasing inequality in the distribution of resources)—as 'the propagation of the new at the lowest human cost, and optimal speed, in a network of relations whose viewpoint becomes universalised'.[1]

It is true that this is only the view of an economist, though of one who is very concerned about the social and human repercussions of economic transformations. But the language of anthropology is not very different. When Ruopp, for example, defines what he understands by 'development' for a given community, it is utilitarian ends that he emphasises. And if he includes moral ends, it is to the degree that these supply an infra-structure, this time a mental one, for economic change.[2] We have not come very far from Perroux who defines development in terms of mental changes as well as by social change. The ends proposed by Ruopp are, in effect, the following:

—increased control over the national environment;
—increased control over the social environment;
—increased control of individuals over themselves;

—increased cooperation among men within the society and increased cooperation between that society and others;
—finally, increased individual freedom in these cooperative relations, that is a progressive passage from the biological to the ethical, the ensemble of controls we have enumerated having to serve moral ends.

But which moral ends? If two of them are cited—cooperation and individualism—they are also closely linked with each other. Cooperation is only envisaged in the form of mutual aid between autonomous and independent individuals, or in the form Durkheim called 'organic solidarity' (as opposed to mechanical solidarity) which is precisely that of primitive or peasant societies. Ruopp's notion thus finally postulates the imposition from without of a form of morality which is our own, but which is not general. For the only universality possible for moral law, as Kant clearly saw, is that of pure 'form'; each society distinguishes between what is 'obligatory' and what is 'forbidden', but the content of that distinction varies from one people to another. This is particularly true of individualism. Individualism is certainly a moral quality required for the smooth functioning of a capitalist economy, but which becomes a vice for all economies based on other criteria. We know that for Comte among others, it was even the supreme vice, a fruit of human conceit. As he was fond of saying, 'no one has any other right than to do his duty'.

In these circumstances, does the anthropologist have the right to impose his preferences and value system on other peoples than his own? Sol Tax thinks not. For his part and from this point of view he carefully distinguishes the sphere of knowledge from that of politics.[3] Even though the reasoning which links the end or goal of each act with the means used to realise it belongs to science, the *choice* of an end or goal belongs to politics. And politics is not a science, since there is no science of ends. It consists in utilising the results of anthropological research with a view to realising certain aims, which the government chooses, related to certain values, those which the government has also chosen. 'Science is instrumental.' But this instrument can be utilised by the administration in question in three different ways.

Before leaving to work in the midst of a given population, the administrator can gather together all the anthropological literature about it that exists. Before leaving, he can also receive anthropological training. It may be remembered that this was Malinowski's solution, introducing instruction in ethnology in English schools of colonial administration. France was to follow suit, introducing such instruction in its School of Administration of Overseas Territories. Finally, and this is the third possible solution, the one which permits the best collaboration between science and politics, each staying in its own sphere (knowledge and action, respectively), is that the administrator can employ an anthropologist or a multi-disciplinary team to help him.

In this last solution which concerns us in this chapter, the anthropologist leaves his ivory tower. But doing so, does he not sell his knowledge to profit either national or class interests? Will he not be obliged to limit his observations in terms of their utilisation toward a goal or an end whose hidden spring he does not know? Will he not be forced to set aside a whole series of facts, though they are thrilling, to limit himself to a given sphere, one delimited by others? From then on, since he sells his skill, will he not make anthropology into a 'great whore'? (This term has frequently been used, and is not too strong.)

One may say that American anthropology has been beset by this problem. It tried to fight on two fronts at once—against the ivory tower, which is the renunciation of action, and against the prostitution of the scholar. It tried to manoeuvre between this Charybdis and this Scylla to escape the clutches of both. J. F. Embree and Sol Tax, to cite only these defenders of applied anthropology, give analogous answers, though in slightly different forms.

The professional, says the former, must observe certain moral principles. Just as the doctor takes as his mission the curing of sick people who come to consult him about their health, so the anthropologist has a mission—a noble mission—to fulfil: to prevent friction between men, eliminate violence in social relations, protect the rights and dignity of groups to be administered.[4] For his part, Tax notes that the anthropologist is not merely a technician, but a man. As a technician, he has skills which enable him to work toward the realisation of certain ends. But as a man he has the freedom and thus the duty to reject all demands which seem to him morally unjustifiable. He can, for example, accept a policy scheme which allows reconciliation of groups in conflict, and the institution of peaceful relations where before violence reigned. He can refuse on the other hand a policy scheme of forced displacement of a population from one region to another, even if it is intended to take them from an exhausted environment to one richer in resources, if he judges that the social costs of this displacement will be higher than its economic rewards.

The anthropologist is a citizen like the rest, and every citizen has the right to create a philosophy by which he regulates his own conduct, and which defines right and wrong for him.

Tax goes even further, in the direction we indicated in the last chapter which leads ethnology from cultural relativism to a return toward ethnocentrism. Science studies the values and goals of a culture but is, in itself, indifferent. This is perfectly true. But the anthropologist may rightly, by empathy, adopt in one way or another the values as well as the goals of the culture he studies in order to frame his action according to a *pattern* which his observations lead him to see. Tax does not accept this outlook. For him, the citizen-anthropologist draws his values, which guide his manipulation of men and of things, from another source than his science —that is, from his personal philosophy. He even believes that the anthropologist-citizen's social philosophy is more valid if he takes account, unlike the politician or administrator, of social and cultural phenomena obtained through the use of social science.

Briefly, at this point in his argument, it is as though the idea of science wends its way into Tax's mind, and changes from one of objective knowledge to one of social philosophy, since for the scholar the latter is always based on, and proceeds according to, a scientific way of thought. In any case, the anthropologist cannot remain content to elaborate means, he can and must if necessary also give advice on the ends to be sought, to the administrator who employs him. He must do this if not as a scholar, then as a citizen-philosopher, scientifically schooled.[5]

But have we got very far passing in this way from a collective subjectivity (that of the morality of the dominant group) to an individual subjectivity (that of the philosophical ethics of the scholar)? We do not think so. First, because even if these ethics are those of a scholar, and may thus appear somewhat scientific, ethics are not science, but belong to philosophy. All that may be said is that his are more considered than those of others, but we cannot go further than that. Secondly, precisely because the scholar is a man, and all men are fashioned by their milieu, this citizen's philosophy is merely an extension of that of the group to which he belongs, and into which he has been socialised. In the end, this makes him judge the administrator's goals in terms of the scale of values of his own industrial and Christian civilisation which he has internalised. Doubtless, and it is this that should be retained from the preceding paragraph, he is always free to refuse those demands which in his interior tribunal seem unjust to him, dictated either by the national or class interests of the administrator who wants to employ him. But he has inherited his sense of social justice from his culture, and if fortunately it can serve him in opposing certain forms of social inequality, it cannot answer all the questions that the administrator will put to him.

Certain governments, more concerned with avoiding trauma, can oppose too radical change which would overturn traditional structures, preferring more localised and slower reform. Others, more concerned with rapid progress, can seek in-depth mutations. Ethics are not involved here, except if this conservatism or this 'mutationism', rather than meeting the general needs of the people, will only profit a small interest-group. We would say then with Embree and Tax that the morality of the anthropologist-citizen is of great importance. But the problem remains untouched so long as there is not—and there cannot be—a science of ends, or a scientific morality.

The sociology of knowledge has insisted too strongly on the

dual fact that man puts himself into what he does, with his ideas as well as his interests, albeit unconscious ones, and that these ideas and interests are those of the country, social class, or professional group to which he belongs. So that we must further discuss that ethnocentrism of the whites which brings liberal democracy with it, as a superior form suitable for all humanity. But just as we seem to reach an impasse, the solution, or at least the beginning of one, comes to light. For it is a fact that, as they become independent, countries wish to become industrialised, participate in technological advances, raise the standard of living of their peoples.

It is a fact that—as Lalande observed clearly before the wars that shook our continent—if the law of evolution was primarily the law of progressive differentiation, we have entered a new era, that of involution as opposed to evolution; that is of the progressive 'uniformisation' of all humanity. And this involution occurs according to the Western model, seen as the superior one. Thus there is a diffusion of the same values, which are our own values— European or American—of democracy and technological progress. Which in turn facilitates the dialogue between the administrators and the anthropologist. Citizens of different countries, men of action or men of science, have about the same philosophy, the same general world view.

Doubtless, this movement toward commonality of representations and beliefs is slowing down today. Reaction is setting in. We still speak of development, but of cultural pluralism in the directions development will take. Asia was always proud of her cultures. But Francophonic Africa, with its ideology of negritude, and Anglophonic Africa, with its theory of African personality, are more and more concerned to lose none of those spiritual values which are their own and which are endangered by too servile an imitation of the West.

Africanisation of groups is achieved by an Africanisation of applied anthropology. For only the black anthropologist will be capable of developing his country with respect for its indigenous culture, and of finding roads toward the necessary conciliation between new ends and tradition inherited from the ancestors. Still, this African applied anthropology—as yet more a hope than a reality—is placed in the humanist framework, of a humanism extended to the limits of humanity and not those of Western culture, where all peoples contribute the fruits of their respective cultures to the communal feast of Man. This results in the continuation of the dialogue, even during this phase of reaction, first among anthropologists themselves and, secondly, between the ensemble of anthropologists and the governments or administrations that require their services.

We must go still further and state that during this phase of reaction, the dialogue of governors with anthropologists is easier than that with other specialists—economists, nutritionists, sociologists, or psychologists—because anthropologists begin with a knowledge of ethnic or national cultures, their differences and their original features. The others, however, are more preoccupied with the most general and banal aspects of human nature. One could devote a whole chapter to the errors made by specialists when they are not enlightened by the anthropologists, and to their failures. But we shall not write it; we shall content ourselves with a few examples.

Firstly, that of the case of the economists' disquiet when they have to accept that the models of economic growth that they had elaborated according to what had happened or was happening in Europe or America did not work in the Third World. Granted, they started with simple solutions, which allowed them to retain their conviction that these mathematical models were universally valid—one need only adapt them to changing circumstances and new situations without changing them or complicating them only to the extent of taking account of other variables.

But as Furtado[6] has skilfully shown in the case of Brazil, it is not a matter of adapting or complicating the models but of finding new and non-generalisable ones—which implies a recognition of cultural multiplicity.

White international experts during a trip to West Africa were unpleasantly struck by the strong smell of dried fish—the nutritional base of certain groups and a medium of exchange between fishermen and cultivators. So they deodorised the fish, with the result that these groups stopped eating them and thus deprived themselves of their only protein source. These nutritionists had merely forgotten that European taste is determined by Western culture and is not 'natural' or 'universal'; that nothing is so relative as the appreciation of smells, savours and tastes.

Psychiatrists introduced not only their nosology but also their therapeutic techniques into Africa, before observing that at least with some types of mental illness traditional healers had more success than they. For Western psychiatry heals the individual, and in Africa the individual does not exist except in and through the family; the disorganised family must be rebuilt and its unity re-established for the individual to be cured. Thus, little by little, the anthropologist was led to become the master of ceremonies (*maître de jeu*), to advise and to direct, by centering change around each culture in terms of its own ends and values.

A curious thing: the white anthropologist is more often pre-occupied with this relativity of civilisations, requiring the discovery of original solutions, than is the native politician or the coloured anthropologist. Sometimes it seems to the latter, who have studied at Western universities, that the ethnologist—by stressing the importance of cultural diversity and the need to respect it—remains a 'colonialist' or a 'neo-colonialist' wishing to delay progress rather than speed it, so as to maintain the superiority of the white world and the dependence of the former colonies, now independent.

During international congresses or colloquia we have been struck by this contrast between Western anthropologists, who are restrained and tolerant, and African specialists trained in Europe or the United States, who are intransigent and radical in their projects for reform to the point of being—in these scholarly reunions —often the only advocates of this Western 'ethnocentrism' which they internalised and made their own during their university days. Whereas ethnology and the sociology of knowledge have already profoundly marked anthropologists, European even more than American, forcing them to achieve a critical rather than a dogmatic conception of reason and of science.

Thus, in the realm of ends, dialogue is translated by the expression of opposition as well as of cooperation. The ends of administrators are political and those of anthropologists moral—respectively the ends of demiurgic desires for change and those of traditional societies. And as well, there is the dilemma of the ivory tower versus 'prostitution' as aspects of the fundamental role which the anthropologist should play in today's world.

NOTES

1. F. Perroux, *Économie du XXᵉ siècle*, Presses Universitaires de France, Paris, 1961, Chap. III.
2. P. Ruopp, *Approaches to Community Development*, Mouton, The Hague, 1953.
3. Sol Tax, 'Anthropology and Administration', *Amer. Indigena*, V, 1941.
4. J. F. Embree, 'Applied Anthropology and Its Relationship to Anthropology', *Amer. Anthrop.*, 47, 1945.
5. Sol Tax, op. cit.
6. C. Furtado, *Le Brésil à l'Heure du Choix*, Plon, Paris, 1964.

What a Scientific Theory of Acculturation can bring to Applied Anthropology 3

Obviously if the anthropologist acts with an end in view, be it a personal one or one dictated from outside, there is still no science of ends. May there then be a science of means? If so, naturally the latter can only emerge empirically from research, and this research will cover the effects of contacts and inter-penetrations between different cultures or civilisations. As we said to begin with, applied anthropology was born from studies of acculturation, even if later it enlarged its scope; it appeared when acculturation became planned instead of free. Before proceeding further, we must ask ourselves then what contributions a theory or theories of acculturation will bring to the formation of an applied anthropology worthy of the name.

Elsewhere we have explored the problems of acculturation themselves sufficiently not to return to them here.[1] To do so would take us beyond the scope of this book. Here we must be content to use the famous definition from Redfield, Linton and Herskovits' *Memorandum:*

'Acculturation comprehends those phenomena which result when groups of individuals having different cultures come into continuous first-hand contact, with subsequent changes in the original culture patterns of either or both groups. Under this definition, acculturation is to be distinguished from culture-change, of which it is but one aspect, and as-similation, which is at times a phase of acculturation. It is also to be differentiated from diffusion, which, while occurring in all instances of acculturation, is not only a phenomenon which frequently takes place without the occurrence of the

37

types of contact between peoples specified in the definition given above, but also constitutes only one aspect of the process of acculturation.'[2]

We may add that diffusion involves the existence of a transfer which is 'terminated' while acculturation involves change which is still taking place. 'Culture contact' (the phrase preferred by the British to the American 'acculturation', but which covers approximately the same range of facts) 'has to be regarded', says Fortes, 'not as a transfer of elements from one culture to another, but as a continuous process of interaction between groups of different culture.'[3] We must add two further major distinctions. The first, to which we shall return below, separates acculturation from enculturation. Enculturation takes place during the first years of life; it consists in the transmission of culture from adults to the succeeding generation. Acculturation, on the other hand, involves adults already enculturated by their parents, and it is precisely because it involves already-formed adults (Kardiner would say those who have already a formally based personality) that it is problematic, creates conflicts in the individual psyche, and rarely leads to true assimilation.[4]

The second distinction is that which must be established between a cultural process—acculturation, and a sociological process—integration. Doubtless, integration (of a minority group with a nation or state or, in the case of the new African nations, of one ethnicity or one tribe with the global society) is facilitated by a preliminary homogenisation of the two cultures in contact. It is nonetheless true that one can well imagine an integration of two groups or cultures into a single whole politically or economically integrated, without these groups losing their native cultures or changing them. Indigenous Mexican policy took as its ideal task the integration of Indian communities into the nation without touching their own cultures.[5] And we know that the role of the great international bodies, the League of Nations and the United Nations Organisation has been to prevent the multi-ethnic states of Europe from making a criminal attack on the civilisations of minority groups on the pretext of their better integration without at the same time, however, permitting the latter to secede politically or reform themselves economically.

The study of acculturation should further include that of non-cultural phenomena which have an *a posteriori* effect on culture change. Ecological phenomena come first. We know the importance of the environment for man—Australian desert, tropical forest, circumpolar icecaps. To live man must adapt to his milieu, and one may to a certain extent define culture as the set of 'responses', the adaptation of man to his environment. But the Westerner may, through his technology, without having contact with the native, bring about important changes in this environment and thus even modify the relationship between man and nature. Culture change, necessitated by new responses to a transformed ecological system, does not derive directly from contact but from the transformation worked on the environment.

Demographic phenomena follow in importance. In stressing the importance of this factor we are not concerned with the number of individuals; we know that the phrase 'ethnic minority' is very ambiguous. In fact, in many multi-racial societies the so-called ethnic minority is actually demographically a majority. This term 'minority' has only the semantic value given it by politics; it in fact denotes the politically dominated population. Rather, in speaking of demography we are alluding to population structures.

A classic example is that which the Americans call the 'masculine frontier'. We know that in tropical countries, males generally migrate alone; and this irruption of males will have a different influence according to whether the recipient population, where they must find sexual partners, is formed of exogamous matrilineal or patrilineal clans. Culture contact is then structured from without by demographic structures, in this case sexual ones. (Elsewhere, for example in the case of 'forced labour' it is a question of 'age classes' within which these contacts must operate.)

Acculturation thus defined and delimited, gave rise especially in the first part of the twentieth century to numerous monographic or theoretical studies. But the concern was either with creating a conceptual scheme of references (whose different terms—conflict, adjustment, interpenetration, syncretism, counter-acculturation, etc., became more and more refined) or with formulating a typology, that of 'situations' in which these interpenetrations of civilisations occur, postulating that it is the sociological situations (slavist, colonial, etc.) which determine the nature of the processes of culture change. Whether one leans more, as in the USA, toward systems of reference, or, as in France, e.g., with Balandier, toward situations, it is clear that applied anthropology will profit to a certain if rather limited extent.

In order that works on acculturation may provide a solid foundation for an applied anthropology seen as a 'science of means', we must be able, by the comparative method, to draw from them a certain number of formal laws independent of the different cultural contents which exist, and transcending environmental diversities and historical conjunctions. Parsons thus affirms à propos the social dynamic (of which acculturation is one phase, the second being that involving internal innovations) that there are regularities only in synchrony. His famous theory of 'action' does not apply to diachronic facts.

To make his ideas more understandable, he compares social sciences to biological sciences. If there are laws in biology, those of the functioning of life, there are on the other hand no such laws in what we are accustomed to call the 'natural sciences'—in zoology and botany where each species, animal or vegetable, can be the object of description but not of a general theory. In the same way, all that we can do for the phenomena of the social or cultural dynamic is to provide empirical description and, at the outside, to establish typologies.[6] We do not, and we cannot, attain the sphere of laws. But Parsons' opinion is not shared by all scholars, and it surely seems that we can find a certain number of sufficiently general regularities[7] so that applied anthropology can profit by them, in comparing the many monographs dealing with these acculturative processes.

But before enumerating these regularities which will form the main part of this chapter, we must first make two further preliminary points. The first is that by choice we will use the term 'regularities' rather than 'laws', though some readers may find the former rather vague. Without entering into a discussion about the existence of true laws in the human sciences, or even of 'tendential laws,' all we can say is that there is a sociological or anthropological determinism and that the social engineer who wishes to manipulate reality to bend it to his ends must take this into account, as it forms both a brake on his thaumaturgic power and a springboard to a system of rational action. But we cannot go further and measure the exact 'weight' of this determinism.

The second point is that in our view there are three types of contact: 'free,' 'forced'—of which the colonial situation provides the best example—and finally 'planned,' which brings us to applied anthropology. Most of the regularities which we will enumerate have been taken from the comparison of monographs dealing with 'free' or nearly-free contacts since it seemed that the less human will intervened, the more the play of determinism must become apparent. It will be necessary thereafter to proceed from these free acculturations to controlled and planned ones, to see if we will find the same regularities or even other new ones.

The first observation to be made which will serve as a point of departure, is that it is never cultures which are in contact but rather individuals. If we take the 'donor' individuals, it is clear that whoever they may be—colonists, missionaries, adventurers—they never represent the totality of their cultures but only the part which Linton would call 'statutory', that is, the sector of their cultures which bears on their distinctive statuses and roles in the global society. This means that on the recipients' part whole elements of their native culture are not touched. As Parsons says of the Mexican community of Mitla, 'certain elements may be preserved simply through ignorance of anything different; in other words, certain parts of the two cultures in contact cannot be in contact at all.' It is only over time when the number of individuals increases (and with them there is an increase in the various sectors of the donor culture) and when contacts are continuous that the recipient culture can be reached in its entirety.

However, here as well the recipient culture is only an anthropological abstraction. What exists in fact are individuals who have different statuses and roles, with specific attitudes, behavioural norms and interests—men and women, elders and juniors, political chiefs and sorcerers, free people and people of caste. Certain of these individuals may find it profitable to accept the traits of a given culture; others on the contrary will see in them a grave danger to their prestige or authority. Which means that certain borrowed traits may not extend beyond one sector of the recipient culture, e.g., women or caste groups, and remain encysted in that sector, without reaching the mass, while others, because borrowed by political leaders, may spread.

It would seem that this first observation is very important for applied anthropology, for, here as well, it will be individuals and not, properly speaking, their cultures who will be in contact. Specialists in applied anthropology have clearly seen this and attempt to discover within all communities the leaders capable of transforming the mass taking themselves as starting points. We shall have to return more fully to this point later, for if all are in agreement concerning the principle, they do not agree as to the identification of 'real' leaders. It must be added that it is perhaps not so much the prestige of certain individuals that is most important as their placement in the social structure.[8] That is, ideological networks are worth more consideration than are psychological elements such as personal prestige and charismatic gifts. And above all, if applied anthropology takes account of individuals in the recipient culture, it does not seem preoccupied by those in the donor culture—specialised experts, educators, or others who are assumed to represent the totality of their civilisation while in fact they always represent only one sector or social class—generally the lower-middle class and sometimes the members of it who are maladjusted in their country of origin.

If we now proceed from specific individuals to the cultures which they bring with them and which at first sight we would consider analytically not as organised *gestalts* but as sets of culture traits, a certain number of regularities may be found: non-sym-

bolic elements—technical and material—are more easily transferred than are symbolic elements, e.g., religious or scientific. The
simplicity of a culture trait facilitates its transfer: its complexity
retards it. Tools for example are diffused faster than machines
whose use by natives is more complicated and requires a longer
apprenticeship. Finally, if we distinguish within all culture traits a
form—their manifest expression which is to some extent visible—
and a function, the set of needs they satisfy, their meaning, the
ensemble of mental associations, of images or ideas which are
grouped around them,[9] then both the number and the richness of
the observable regularities in the acculturation process also increase:

   1. The more 'foreign' the form of a culture trait and thus the
farther removed from those of the recipient culture, the more difficult will be its acceptance as this culture trait cannot be reinterpreted in the recipient culture's terms. This does not mean, however,
that it may not sometimes be accepted; but if it is, it will be as an
'imitation' or 'addition' not as a 'substitution' or a 'replacement'.
Briefly, it remains floating on the periphery. It is not taken up—
'eaten' or 'digested'—it has not a dynamic value for the profound
transformation or mentalities or sensibilities.

   2. Forms are more readily transferable than are functions; we
have already suggested this when we spoke of functionalism in the
historical chapter. Malinowski correctly sought to persuade
colonisers that they would not succeed in imposing new institutions
unless they were more suitable in their formal advantages, for
fulfilling the same functions as the old ones that they were meant
to replace. We agree completely; and we have given the example
of the piped water supply. However, Barnett observes that functional equivalents introduced into a culture rarely replace the old
institutions. Doubtless, they are incorporated into it but as 'alternative modes' of satisfying the same needs. The old institution
remains through inertia as do old habits, alongside the new. The
two functional equivalents are not then interchangeable. This may
sometimes have serious consequences. For the existence of dual or
alternative means of doing the same thing means that the be-

haviour of one individual or another, in a given situation will no longer be predictable since there is freedom of choice and not, as before, behaviour imposed by the group. This unforeseeability is a factor for confusion in the mind which is then often transferred to the affective level as anxiety, which is thus one of the specific pathological phenomena of both free and forced acculturation— perhaps even as we shall see, of planned acculturation.

3. A culture trait, whatever its form and function, will be all the better received and integrated if it can take on a semantic value which harmonises with the field of meanings of the recipient culture. That is, it will be reinterpreted. Or, if you prefer, the natives must recognise certain of their own ideas in the new system of change which is proposed to them not only in order that it be accepted, but that it may become effectual. Eaton has termed 'controlled acculturation' the process by which a culture accepts the practice of another by integrating it into its own value system.[10] This term is easily confused with 'organised', 'directed' and 'planned' acculturation. We prefer Herskovits' term, that of 're-interpretation', which he terms the integration of new culture traits by 'adjustment' to the recipient culture. The concept of re-interpretation is at any rate richer than that of controlled acculturation, for it also includes the 'process by which old meanings are attributed to new elements' and that by which 'new values change the cultural significance of old forms'.

We have given examples of these two mechanisms elsewhere[11] and emphasised their importance both in the work of Durkheim (the superiority of internal causation over external causation)[12] and in that of Boas who defined acculturation as the way 'in which foreign elements are remodelled according to the patterns prevalent in their new environment' and who, as a result, demands of the ethnographer concerned with this sort of problem that he investigate primarily the 'internal forces' of culture 'which remodel external elements according to the patterns' belonging to that culture.[13] This 'golden rule' of theoretical anthropology should also be that of applied anthropology.

Thus far we have only traced those regularities involving

isolated culture traits. However, as we pursue our inventory of regularities, particularly when we arrive at the concept of re-interpretation, we have imperceptibly proceeded from the point of view which defines culture as a set of traits to that which sees it as a system. The analytical approach that we have been following cannot effectively lead us very far toward the formation of an applied anthropology since by making of borrowing, to use Fortes' expression, a matter of elements 'mechanically pitchforked like bundles of hay' from one culture to another, we forget that every culture constitutes a *gestalt*, that is, an organised and structured unity.[14]

It may be said that the progress of acculturation studies from American cultural anthropology to British social anthropology—which though giving, according to various authors, different senses to the words 'structure' and 'organisation' has always at least given primary importance to these notions—is marked at the methodological level by a parallel progress from the 'holistic' to the 'analytic' approach. All elements of a society are articulated one to another in such a fashion that the study of contact, to be valid and to be able to offer a model of man's modifying action, must always concern sets and not particular traits. Here again, from this new perspective, regularities may be found.

Firstly there is that of chain reactions.[15] Since everything in a culture is bound together, it suffices to modify one of its elements for that first modification to bring about others, often unforeseen, and for the whole equilibrium of the global society finally to be affected by it. All the sectors articulated to each other must re-arrange themselves so that society will find a new equilibrium; but this new equilibrium will be different from the old one. Further, at the beginning one need only influence one culture ele-ment, which might seem relatively neutral or peripheral vis-à-vis the 'culture base' of a people (what the people themselves con-sider most important; for example, one may have introduced agricultural machinery to lighten the labour of peasants using hoe cultivation) and behold, the whole family structure, extended family or lineage will become disorganised. Or else one introduces currency to facilitate and generalise economic exchange and suddenly, in consequence, the old alliance system is transformed. Marriage by compensation and gifts becomes marriage by buying spouses, while the control of elders as givers of women to their juniors is destroyed.

Before bringing any modification to a cultural and social system, applied anthropology must foresee the continuing series of chain reactions which will follow for the whole of the system; in brief, it must progress from a short-term view of the effects of its manipulations to a long-term one.

The consideration of culture as an organised totality also permits the economist who wishes to apply Western models to other societies to pluralise his concept of 'rationality'. As Godelier states, 'one must start from structures, their relationships and their exact roles, to grasp the rationality of individual behaviour.' Social and cultural systems are not illogical; they merely obey a different logic from our own. Conspicuous consumption, for example, which irritates those who wish to introduce a capitalist mentality into a pre-industrial society is not an irrational element to be destroyed.

> 'By means of this global social rationality, discovered through anthropological analysis, economic mechanisms may be reinterpreted and better understood. Conduct which seems irrational to us regains its own rationality when placed in the context of the functioning of the whole society. Today's rationality may be tomorrow's irrationality. The rational of one society may be the irrational of another; finally, there is no purely economic rationality.'[16]

Thus what seems reasonable to the planner, that which he sees rejected all the same because of the inextricable link between the social and the economic, should turn applied anthropology toward two new tasks. In the first place, toward the comprehension of the behaviour of the 'decider' vis-à-vis that of the 'advisor' —so-called rational behaviour. In the second place, toward a search—beyond action which would be purely economic, which assumes that development occurs spontaneously through the play of economic forces—for a strategy which on the contrary would be extra-economic and which would begin by acting on other elements of the social system. The Russians first acted on the basis of political domination. And we know that the students of Latin America consider that their revolutionary movements are infinitely more effective for the under-developed economies of their continent than the programme of economic experts for community development.

But we believe that the main import of the holistic or globalistic approach to acculturation is to make us understand the phenomenon of resistance as a cultural defence mechanism against influences coming from without and which threaten both the equilibrium of the society and the affective security of its members. This tenacious, crafty, or violent resistance to the action of social engineers and planners, this systematic refusal to be receptive to these people who, after all, 'have no vested interest in the affair', who 'only want the best for the natives' or the peasant masses, has often shocked and discouraged the former. And all the more since they most often are not anthropologists and see it as an invasion of the irrational.[17]

If we have rightly cited Godelier above, it is precisely because he points up the ethnocentric character of our notion of 'rationality'—that what is resisting it is another rationale, rooted in a certain structure of social relations. Even though the planner talks about an upsurge of irrationality in the face of his 'reasonable' and 'beneficent' projects, it is in fact a matter of the social reformer's ignorance of the stratified levels of the sociological reality, as Gurvitch has skilfully pointed out.

For alongside the 'global society' which is structured and organised, and consequently alongside the 'collisions' between different social and cultural systems, one must also take into account what Mauss called 'total phenomena'—those phenomena which Gurvitch studied in depth in his sociology—to reveal their layered, stratified nature. Besides, alongside collisions between systems, account must be taken as well of conflicts between these multiple levels of social reality or, if you prefer, of the revolt of these deeper layers against the mutations which one causes the superficial ones to undergo.

Berque emphasised these irruptions of spontaneous forces from 'natural man' against the constraining or deteriorating aspects of development to the extent that they tend toward the abolition of ethnic or collective personalities. Certainly, he did not deny the necessity of development and he even condemned traditionalism once it has become only a degeneration of original traditions: 'traditionalism should be repudiated not because it retains the old-fashioned but because it corrupts and exploits it.' At the least he demands of applied anthropology that it have recourse to the internal, to continuities (as opposed to cultural discontinuities introduced by change), to the authentic, the original or, if you will, the immortal.[18] We thus hold to the two basic reasons for resistance to change, the one which is due to the opposition of social systems in contact and the other which results from the patchwork of extraneous models and which, because these dissociate personal ethnic identities, tears at a certain point under the strain of internal and original forces. 'What doth it profit a man to gain the whole world if he loseth his own soul?'

Theoretical anthropology distinguishes two forms of opposition—resistance which occurs at the beginning of the acculturative process and counter-acculturation, which occurs at its final stage. Resistance is not in fact the absence of a propensity for change—as certain people would have it in their naive optimism and their more or less unconscious desire to minimise its significance—rather it is an active refusal to change. The inhabitants of Montawai Island, near Sumatra, refused to take over rice cultivation from the neighbouring Malay, even though such cultivation would have allowed them to improve their standard of living, because it requires continuous labour while their own religion demands a break of several months without work. Hindus allow themselves to die of starvation near their sacred cows which could save their lives but which their beliefs forbid them to slaughter.

At the beginning of this chapter we distinguished acculturation from enculturation. Now we may say that enculturation is precisely what prevents or poses obstacles to the acculturative process. A personality shaped from tenderest infancy according to the norms of the reigning culture, having internalised the values and ideas of its ethnicity, feels threatened both in its identity and in its unity by new norms and values that one wishes to impose on it; and this is perfectly natural.

For the moment we will take up only this source of resistance. We will encounter others when we proceed from free to forced acculturation. Counter-acculturation, which takes the forms of 'nativism,' 'prophetism,' 'messianism,' and 'millenarianism' appears when acculturation has already begun and when individuals realise its destructive and disorganisational effects on their ethnic personality. These are attempts at turning back and at re-tribalisation. Applied anthropology fears them for these movements seem to prove that it is never sure to succeed, that a tidal wave risks destroying at one blow the edifice it has built and which then seems merely a sandcastle, washed away by the violence of monstrous waves. It will then be necessary to start from scratch.

Yet these movements, far from being fearsome, should on the contrary be reassuring. Revolt is a sign of domesticated change. Messianism or millenarianism are 'syncretic' movements which generally comprise an ensemble of Christian and traditional beliefs and, as a result—to re-establish the social equilibrium destroyed by the missionaries—attempt to include Christian principles in the indigenous culture rather than throw them out.[19] Cargo cults prove the acceptance on the part of the Melanesians of Western goods. They only show an ignorance of the appropriate techniques for producing them. Here again we may ask ourselves if opposition, like resistance, does not come as much from the encounter of the two antagonistic normative systems as from the fact that the cultural assimilation once begun was not followed by the integration of the native into the dominant group's society on an equal footing, which in turn causes us to proceed from free to forced acculturation.[20]

Devereux and Loeb have given the name 'antagonistic acculturation' to this set of refusals and of turnings-back, and they also
distinguish two types: resistance to borrowing and resistance to
the borrower. But in addition, they emphasise, alongside the
jealous concern of each group to maintain its own uniqueness, the
fact that each culture has its own modes of adaptation to existing
problems and that these adaptive modes are inapplicable to the
entirely new puzzles posed by contact. From which emerge the
feelings of insecurity of individuals which are transposed into a
defensive isolationism or which first stick to negation—whilst
they are influenced all the same and modified—and then their
identity feels threatened and resorts to regression, that is, to a
return to the models of behaviour common before contact.[21]

Inter-cultural ethnology then confronts us with a certain number of observations of tendencies and regularities that applied
anthropology can use, whether for isolated 'culture traits' or for
cultures viewed as functional systems. But there are still two points
to consider. If cultures form systems, these systems are not always
and completely coherent. The anthropologist must beware of a
sort of 'Rousseauism' which sees harmony and equilibrium everywhere.

Secondly, cultural systems are not static; there is nowhere a
'people without history'. The anthropologist must, if not re-
constitute a chronology of culture, which is most often impossible,
at least take account, alongside the static, of the forces of change,
the evolution of cultural systems. And these two points are of
great significance for applied anthropology.

Contemporary ethnology recognises the omnipresent existence
of internal contradictions—and not only in our own capitalist
societies—contradictions in kinship and authority systems, or
between them. That, as well as centripetal forces—of social
cohesion and control of individuals by collective norms—there
are also centrifugal forces at play which though less powerful
(otherwise society would fall apart) tend towards the disaggregation of the system. Contemporary British social anthropology
has definitively established that, to survive, all cultures behave as

sluice gates of liberation for these centrifugal forces while at the same time they take them in hand to limit their effects or to make them serve in the end that cohesion which they are in danger of undermining. Examples are: compensatory ceremonies and 'rituals of rebellion'—of women against men, servants against masters subjects against their political leaders.

It is clear that applied anthropology must pay special attention to these rituals of rebellion and their analysis, since they manifest what may be called weak points of the system one wishes to change, symptomatic of internal tensions and latent contradictions, into which the social engineer can insinuate himself to realise the goals he has given himself, or that he has been given, much more easily and effectively than if he tried to fight directly against the whole system.

The old ethnology seemed to postulate that all traditional cultures were static, and that consequently all changes in them could only be exogenous in origin. Today we recognise that all culture contact occurs between dynamic cultures, each caught up in motion characteristic of it. This idea, first brought forth by Sapir in the linguistic sphere ('Language changes over time in a traced current. It has a tendency.'[22]) was then generalised to the whole set of facts of civilisation under the name of 'cultural tendency'. And we may say of these cultural tendencies precisely what Sapir says of linguistic ones. We know that each individual changes his culture by living it. But we should be mistaken to think that these individual variations are either neutralised or are capable of acting randomly either in one direction or another. In fact, all these individual variations are cumulative in a given direction; present change is prefigured in past, and is a prelude to future change.

In brief, all cultures change following a trend which points them in a certain direction. Africans, for example, refuse to see in colonisation—that is in an exogenous source—the creation of the political nations of present-day Africa. They hold that the tendency of their societies to progress from local groupings to vast ethnic confederations came well before colonisation, and that the latter only followed a 'trend' already traced by the nature of the great empires of the Sudan, or the kingdoms of the Congo. They maintain that this resulted in the formation of multi-ethnic nationalities. This example suffices to show that applied anthropology cannot succeed except to the extent that its action does not go counter to history, but that it will succeed in following in each particular case the direction of flow of the culture it hopes better to plan.

*   *   *

What distinguishes forced acculturation, whether it be in a situation of slavery or in a colonial one, is that there acculturation is already organised—as it will be in planned acculturation—but in terms of the ends of a given class or stratum, and for its sole profit. This does not mean that this second type of acculturation does not respond to the regularities we have elucidated in studying free acculturation, e.g., conflict of interests. Slavery has always allowed those slaves who became Christians and assimilated themselves to Western culture to profit by certain channels of upward mobility so as to integrate themselves into the dominant system with a status between that of the 'masters' and that of the 'field hands'.

Colonisation made use of 'house slaves' and 'people of caste' to destroy those systems it wanted to overthrow, for example in the case of traditional chiefs, by increasing their power while at the same time reducing them in other spheres to the role of intermediaries between the metropolitan authority and the peasant masses. But this second type of assimilation differs from the first in that it controls the forces for change which it employs instead of allowing the laws of culture contact to act freely. And in so doing it envisages their short-term effects rather than their long-term ones. Thus, forced acculturation is expressed:

(1) by the multiplication of conflicts and

(2) by the intensification of phenomena of disaggregation and the speed of their operation, while free acculturation more slowly allows phenomena of restructuration to operate in a parallel way.

We must say a word about conflict, for it also exists in planned acculturation. All change occurs to the detriment of certain groups which, naturally, resist it. French sociology, with Balandier, has emphasised the importance of conflict. But we must still make sure not to give too much significance to the disorganisational effects of conflict and minimise its organisational effects as a result.

Firstly, these conflicts in effect reveal those intra-community weaknesses and tensions that applied anthropology must know about to be able to remedy. Secondly, violent contradiction between systems in contact, e.g., the culture of the colonisers and that of the colonised, may create favourable conditions for the appearance of new normative images. It thus, to return to a is distinction made above, that they allow, by dissociating resistance to change and resistance to the leaders of change, acceptance of new values by the indigenous population while refusing the imposition of these from without. Becoming political, the struggle allows the insidious insinuation of social and economic transformations into the ancient cultural web, without great traditional resistance, because all opposition is invested in the political field, and there is little strength left for it to act simultaneously in others.

Finally, as Barnett has shown, crises are often the point of departure for important innovations, for a conflict situation cannot continue uninterrupted; it must finally find a solution, and generally a compromise.[23] Basically, in free acculturation conflicts tend to resolve themselves by new adjustments; it is only when the donor culture keeps up a constant pressure for assimilation—no matter the cost—of the minority of the victor, and consequently allows these conflicts one sole solution, that imposed from without, that we encounter those destructive acculturation situations of which we must now speak.

The facts are too well-known for it to be useful to underline them—revolt of youth against parents, increase in the rates of divorce and family disintegration, disappearance of mutual aid, appearance of prostitution and juvenile delinquency in colonial towns, increase of mental illness, disorganisation of subsistence agriculture, rise in sorcery, etc. Today, all specialists agree that if development leads to benefits, there is always a higher or lower price to be paid.

And perhaps one of the main reasons for the emergence of planned acculturation is this agreement, and the desire to develop the so-called under-developed countries 'at the lowest cost'. But this planned acculturation, which will become the objective of applied anthropology, takes different forms or, if you prefer, employs different strategies depending on whether one is concerned with planned acculturation in a capitalist or a socialist context. Since we are now very close to applied anthropology, we will devote the next two chapters to these two forms.

NOTES

1. R. Bastide, *Introduction à l'étude des interprétations des civilisations*, Course at the Sorbonne, 1950. 'Problèmes de l'entrecroisement des civilisations', in *Traité de Sociologie*, G. Gurvitch, II, Presses Universitaires de France, Paris, 1960.
2. M. Redfield, R. Linton, and M. J. Herskovits, *Amer. Anthrop.*, 38, 1936.
3. M. Fortes, 'Culture Contact as a Dynamic Process', *Africa*, 9, 1936.
4. M. J. Herskovits, *Man and his Works*, Alfred Knopf, New York, 1948. Cf. G. Bateson, 'Culture Contact and Schismogenesis', *Man*, 199, 1935.
5. A. Beltram, *El processo de aculturacion*, Mexico, 1957. The best-known example of cultures in contact for generations and which are functionally linked without acculturation having taken place, each of the four societies linked symbiotically, retaining its culture and its language, is that of the Toda (pastoralists), Badaga (agriculturalists), Keta (artisans) and Kerumba (gatherers and sorcerers) given by Mandelbaum in 'Culture Change among the Nilghiri Tribes', *Amer. Anthrop.*, XLIII, pp. 219–26.
6. T. Parsons, *The Theory of Social Action*, The Free Press, Glencoe, 1949.

7. This is the opinion, for example, of H. G. Barnett, 'Culture Processes', *Amer. Anthrop.*, 42, 1940.

8. F. Hawley, 'An Examination of Problems Basic to Acculturation in the Rio Grande Pueblos', *Amer. Anthrop.*, 50, 1948.

9. H. G. Barnett, op. cit.

10. J. W. Eaton, 'Controlled Acculturation: A Survival Technique of the Hutterites', *Amer. Sociol. Rev.*, 17, 1952, pp. 331–40.

11. R. Bastide, 'L'Acculturation formelle', *America Latina*, Rio de Janeiro, VI, 3, 1963.

12. E. Durkheim, *Les Règles de la Méthode Sociologique*, Paris, 1893.

13. F. Boas, 'The Methods of Ethnology', *Amer. Anthrop.*, 22, 1920.

14. M. Fortes, 'Culture Contact as a Dynamic Process', in L. P. Mair (ed.), *Methods of Study of Culture Contact*, London, 1938, p. 62.

15. R. Bastide, 'Causalité interne et causalité externe', *Cahiers Int. de Sociologie*, 21, 1956.

16. M. Godelier, *Rationalité et irrationalité économique*, F. Maspero, Paris, 1966.

17. Lowie: 'But man is not built so as to do the reasonable thing just because it is reasonable. It is far easier for him to do an irrational thing because it has always been done.' Cited in Devereux and Loeb, 'Antagonistic Acculturation', *Amer. Sociol. Rev.*, 8, 1943, pp. 133–48.

18. J. Berque, 'Vers une sociologie des passages', *Études de Sociologie Tunisienne*, I, 1968.

19. R. Bastide, 'Messianisme et dévéloppement économique et social', *Cahiers Int. Sociol.*, XXXI, 1961.

20. On these two forces of opposition to change, endoculturation and the system of domination of one group over another, see G. A. Beltran, 'Espontaneidad y adaptacion en el desarollo de las civilizaciones', *La Palabra y el Hombre*, 29, 1944, pp. 44–53.

21. Devereux and Loeb, op. cit.

22. E. Mandelbaum (ed.), *Selected Writings of Edward Sapir in Language, Culture and Personality*, University of California Press, Berkeley, 1958.

23. H. G. Barnett, 'Personal Conflicts and Cultural Change', *Social Forces*, 20, 1941.

Planned Acculturation in a Capitalist Context 4

Planned acculturation in this context is certainly distinct from free and from forced acculturation. But it is based on all the regularities and established factors we have enumerated in the preceding chapter. That is why we begin with it.[1]

To avoid the pathological effects of forced and destructive acculturation, planned acculturation seeks to develop indigenous communities in accordance with their own traditional norms and ideas. It takes account then of what cultural anthropology has clearly shown—that the individual members of a society all participate in a common world of values, attitudes and interests; that it is these elements that create group coherence and which serve as the basis of solidarity among its members—what Durkheim has called 'mechanical solidarity'.

Therefore one must not try brutally to destroy these traditions or this cultural homogeneity; they must be changed slowly and progressively, causing the recipient group to reinterpret the new values so as to reduce their disruptive force. Certainly, at a given point, the archaic values must be modified as well in so far as they constitute an obstacle to, or a brake on, development. But even then careful account must be taken of psychological data. The individual finds an immediate satisfaction in his present style of life while change—new planting methods for example, or a new diet—cannot bring him any but long-term satisfactions and, first, only worry and anxiety. Thus if one wishes to motivate him to accept new cultivation techniques, or ways of life, one must discover new sorts of immediate satisfactions for him, e.g., to make him feel admired, or to feel himself superior to the mass, etc.

Nevertheless, in general the rule of planned acculturation remains the necessity for foreseeing the effects of innovations introduced, both on individual psyches and on group cohesions. Further, it is to try always to orient change in the direction of traditional values; to inscribe modifications judged beneficial on the former structure of human relations; to present new traits by removing from them as many as possible of the cultural adjuncts that link them with the civilisation that gave rise to them.

For example, when introducing a new type of diet, one more in line with the former one but eliminating its insufficiencies, it should be incorporated into traditional principles, particular ceremonies and the former food ritual. Or, further, for technical agricultural innovations, one should retain the indigenous idea that the earth is not only a source of nourishment but that it has a sacred reality that must be worshipped. Then these new techniques should lose the secular or religiously neutral character that they have in our own civilisation; they should be linked to a cycle of festivals—sowing festivals, harvest festivals, with sacrifices to the Earth Mother—of petitions or thanks.[2] For the earth is a mother that one feeds, with fertiliser, so that it will in its turn feed with the crops it gives forth. Thus to succeed, modern agricultural techniques must be made part of the cycle of prestations and counter-prestations that constitutes one of the essential elements of the so-called 'primitive mentality'.

We can see already, from this first point, that the planner can only succeed if he can count on the collaboration and cooperation of the individual members of the recipient group. But it appears that it is difficult to reach the mass. Leaders must be discovered who will know how to animate the community and orient it toward social or economic progress. We used to believe that first it was necessary to form a progressive minority through education, and that the mass would of itself follow this elite. This was the method already used by the Jesuits who, in a sense abandoning the adults as impossible to change, took their children from them to be educated in their schools and then, once Christianised, sent them back to their families so that they would become teachers to their parents. It was one of the first methods of nativist action programmes in Mexico, which chose among the boys of a village those who seemed most intelligent and raised them in their boarding schools so as to isolate them from the enculturation and influence of the environmental milieu. But this attempt was doomed to fail; these boys of course had been greatly changed, and could no longer live in their old communities, from which they had been spiritually cut off. They swelled the flux of exodus toward the big cities.

This was also the method dear to colonisation—one remembers in France the 'chiefs' schools' of Faidherbe. Here the failure was equally obvious. In fact, what has always happened when one wished first to create an elite was not that the elite served as leavening. It was, on the contrary, scarcely imitated. More simply, a break was produced between the 'évolués' and the 'people'. A new cleavage was introduced into the social solidarity, but it did not at all impel community development.

We shall return later on to this problem, which is of prime importance, and ask ourselves how to discover the real leaders to be recruited, whether these are to be traditional leaders—elders, priests and political chiefs—or whether we should distinguish between 'chiefs' and 'leaders'. For the moment, it is sufficient to note that for a community to choose progress, or what Westerners call progress, it must not be introduced from without. The choice must be made from within and this choice, before becoming a collective one, must first have been made by certain individuals, those who exert or can exert an influence on mass decisions, who may resist or who are likely to take up the reins of command.

However, it will not be enough just to find such men. Planned acculturation as conceived of by Westerners cannot be authoritarian; it follows a democratic model to the point where it considers community enthusiasm more important than the 'machinery' of development. It tries then to create mixed teams comprising traditional elements—members of the old community and new elements, unionists, former students, social workers—to give them all 'team spirit' and to forge these disparate elements into a dynamic whole. It is these teams who will internally develop change techniques and who will reciprocally adapt traditional beliefs to new culture traits.

The method generally adopted is that of 'pilot projects'; change is to be realised by these teams on a limited basis and in a single community. The team not only acts but observes its own creative action. It not only follows the plan given it but modifies it at the same time. And the members from time to time take lessons from the villagers which are drawn from their own behaviour; which means that the experience of community development is no longer the experience of the few, but of all.

The team, though democratically organised if not directed, is at least guided by an ethnologist. For one must know the structure of the culture prior to all manipulation of it. Thus the acculturation is clearly directed but it is still acculturation. Which means that the anthropologist must still have the main voice rather than the sociologist, or the economist, or the politician, or even the nutritionist, doctor or agronomist.

This fundamental point, which should be self-evident from the outset, was unfortunately not foreseen in the course of the first attempts at planned action. It is not even always perceived today, despite the numerous failures of the past. For example, all the measures taken to change the economic structures of Burma, which retarded its productivity, did not succeed because the economic importance of women and youth was neglected. The change-schemes were conceived in terms of our Western conception of the division of labour, while in fact each sex, each age group has a predetermined role and these roles complement each other.

In the same way, if one wishes to reorganize Asian land tenure, account must be taken of the tombs of ghosts, sacred trees and oracles; of the sexual practices of the population as well as of the system of dowries and of succession. Thus, one of the suggestions made by planned acculturation is that a policy that can succeed brilliantly in one country can fail in another. It is unwise to generalise, and one cannot act without a preliminary knowledge of local peculiarities. We shall see, however, that applied anthropology as it has developed does not accept this rule entirely, and we must therefore determine whether it does not have certain limitations.

*   *   *

We shall come to understand better the various processes of directed acculturation if we take two examples from Mexico: one in which a development project was offered from without, and the other in which one was requested from within.

The first, which occurred in 1949 in connection with the Mexican Pilot Project in Basic Education, gathered a team of Mexican educators and specialists to create schools, promote more efficient methods of agricultural production, and improve hygiene and accommodation in a village on the Santiago River. They were also called upon to modify the mentality, attitudes and behaviour of its residents, so as to permit the formation of a cooperative and democratic community capable of profiting from the entire potential of modern technology.[3] As may be seen, of the two groups which would come into contact, one—the donor group—was to intervene actively and intentionally in the culture of the other— the recipient group—seeking a goal that was not recognised by the recipients and was external to them since it was supplied by the Mexican government.

Aside from the director who already had ethnographic experience, the team included an agronomist, a civil engineer, a nurse, a carpenter, a stone mason, a music teacher, all of whom were very patriotic and enthusiastic about the goal they had to achieve. This goal, following the rules of planned acculturation which we have already cited, was even more difficult in this case because the donor group did not have great financial resources. It consisted not in forcing people but in arousing the enthusiasm of the villagers, and in guiding them. The donors only wanted to act as catalysts of local energies.

Here, we shall present on the left the proposals of change which were suggested, and on the right the responses of the community to them:

1. Reorganisation of land tenure, creation of *ejidos*[4].

1. a) Resistance by that section of the population which profited from the old system of land tenure.
b) Passive response by the rest of the population; no manifestation of sentiment either for or against.

2. Introduction of better strains of corn, or breeds of animals; training in better methods of animal husbandry.

2. Aside from the large holders in the area, no favourable response.

3. Change in domestic life via better domestic equipment.

3. Mass apathy.

4. Better sanitation practices.

4. No favourable response either. The only toilets installed remained those at the school. However, it was noted that the villagers started to make greater use of modern medical facilities in the neighbouring town of Santiago, detrimental to traditional medicine. But there was panic fear in face of anti-tuberculosis vaccination.

5. Project to build a cooperative furniture factory.

5. Apparently favourable response. However, those who were trained made furniture only for their own domestic use. No one showed interest in making a commercial profit.

6. Creation of kindergartens.	6. Mothers had to be cajoled into sending their children to them.
7. Creation of a primary school and a night school.	7. Enthusiastic acceptance by a large part of the population.
8. Creation of a teachers' college.	8. Again, enthusiastic reception of the project and pride on the part of the new teachers in the role they were to play.
9. Alignment of the village with the road, and construction of better housing in terms of collective village cooperation.	9. The part of the programme which met with greatest enthusiasm and which was accomplished with the mutual aid of all.
10. Programme of new leisure activities and recreation.	10. Though well received in the town of Santiago, and adopted by neighbouring villages, this failed to take root; the new recreational activities stopped little by little.

11. From the point of view of change of mentality, the individual became more self-aware but (because of the growing anxiety in the face of tempting changes) he also became less fatalistic and more individualistic. But this transformation occurred more among children, through the action of the school, than among adults. The community emerged from its former isolation, became more open to the outside world, and thus placed more value on modern household comforts, and on pleasure (recreational programmes). Above all it came to understand the importance of communal effort, as in the reorganisation and reconstruction of the village along the road, which opened it to the outside world. Individuals

became more aware of their personal rights and more sensitive to injustice.

However, this new consciousness led to new types of conflict which the elders did not know how to resolve; new local committees created by the Mission did not feel strong enough to mediate or to make decisions which would bring peace in the village. Finally, appeal was made to one of the representatives of the Basic Education Project.

As may be seen from this case where change was brought in from outside, only a partial and short-term success could be achieved. What happens then when it is from within that change comes to be required? The example we will consider here is that of Chan Kom, which gave rise to two of Redfield's famous studies.[5]

Chan Kom is one of those villages created by fission from Ebtun, an older, over-populated village. The younger section of the population saw itself as constrained to emigrate to found a colony of Ebtun, a little distance away because of pressure on cultivable land. It should be added that this schism between the parent and colony villages was also due to fighting between antagonistic factions— that the population of Chan Kom, like all schismatic populations, had to continue to recognise the authority of Ebtun, to work for the families of their elders who stayed in the parent village, and having to participate in Ebtun's important festivals, also came to realise their own independence and thus to 'choose for progress' in opposition to Ebtun. We have here a special case of change originating internally—though Chan Kom still had to ask the Mexican government to provide experts and missions, and thus to operate in terms of the same factors of exogenous development.

Independence from Ebtun was gained by administrative reform —Chan Kom had to become a 'pueblo' like the other pueblos of Mexico. In about 1917, the Mayan leaders of the community decided to turn their colony into a village. In 1926 they organised a socialist league, that is, they accepted the notion of progress of the wider nation, as against the communal Indian traditions. For example, they accepted the *ejidal* system of cooperative ownership as against the traditional type of collective ownership, and also the administrative status of the progressive areas of Mexico. The arrival of new families attracted by these reforms led to the building of a Spanish-style village with a central square, perpendicular streets and a school. From that time on, there was a fad that encouraged the inhabitants to want change in everything—dwellings, clothes, life-styles—and to accept progressive behaviour wholeheartedly.

One curious result—given this traditionally Catholic population—was that the progressive fad went so far as the conversion of many Indians to Protestantism, because Protestantism was linked in their minds with ideas of greater material and spiritual progress. It came from the United States—seen as the most developed county in the world—and it symbolised in the minds of the new converts the most radical break with the past that they could imagine.

But administratively, the new pueblo was dependent on the county-seat of the region. So in 1932–3 the inhabitants of Chan Kom fought to gain the status of 'free municipality' for their village. And finally, they succeeded.

Let us stop at this point to evaluate the internal changes which took place during this period. Redfield emphasises the construction of a first mill, since this mill changed the working habits of Indian women, gave them more leisure and thus transformed traditional relations between the sexes. The new houses of Chan Kom, well-built and ranging along streets according to the Hispano-American town model, allowed the appearance and spread of a richer and more extensive style of furnishing, yielding modern comforts.

Progressive abandoning of traditional Indian dress in favour of the Spanish style also symbolised the Indians' entrance into a new world, and their symbolic incorporation into the national community. This change was important for women more than for men: 'a woman who discards the *huipil* in favour of the dress immediately makes a jump upward and outward; after that, she will take up new tasks and new rights, and leave behind her the traditional *jirana* dance and other rustic customs.'

But let us not think that the past was completely exorcised by 'Progress'. Despite the construction of stone houses and their relative comfort, the inhabitants of Chan Kom could not live realistically in them. They ate and passed most of their time outside, and since they were outside and visible, traditional social control mechanisms prevailed. The house could not have its usual sociological influence, that of a change from traditionalism to individualism.

Further, the fact that married sons built their homes near those of their fathers shows clearly that in this period of change, when progress was fashionable, authority remained with the elders, and the nuclear family did not yet separate from the extended family. As for traditional dress, though men did agree to change it since this change was symbolic for them of a modification in their status, they slowed down the movement for their wives. True, girls who went to school wore dresses, but after marriage they most often returned to the *huipil*, because their husbands claimed that dresses were expensive. In fact, it was because women who wore dresses would not work in the fields or gather firewood.

Despite such transformational slow-downs, the social organisation was profoundly modified. New divisions appeared linked to the ecological structure of the Hispano-American town. Houses facing on the square gave their owners greater prestige and greater commercial facilities than those which fronted on the streets. Doubtless, those who lived in the former were the previous leaders of the community, the Tamays, Cemes and Pats, so that the resources of authority and wealth derived both from the past and from the new ecological situation. Yet, we must not minimise the role of the second of these factors in the formation of new hierarchies and a new system of social stratification.

On the other hand, with the formation first of a pueblo then its extension, hitherto unknown forms of the division of labour appeared. Formerly, the colony had only known one traditional form—the sexual division of labour. The only known specialists recognised by the Indians were shaman, prayer-leader, marriage-broker, and wise-woman. There were also traders in almost all traditional Indian communities, but they belonged to a separate class, that of *ladinos*—descendants of Spaniards or half-castes— who were strangers in relation to these communities.

Some of the traditional Indian specialists are still to be found in Chan Kom, e.g., the marriage-broker and the wise-woman. But as well there are now Indians—and not *ladinos*—who are traders or artisans: grocers, masons, carpenters, cattle-traders, etc. Cattle were formerly valued for the prestige they brought to their owner, and agriculture was at a subsistence level. This latter conception of production for domestic consumption has now changed to one of production for personal profit.

When Redfield carried out his investigation, there were about ten merchants in Chan Kom, and the peasants also sold their produce outside. Thus competition was established in the form of competition with regard to a clientele. And it was not limited to this sphere, but also appeared among farmers. Beside the *ejido* there were individually owned plots which tried to expand at the expense of each other. And within the *ejido* itself, the accent was on separate family plots rather than, strictly speaking, on the *ejido* itself, which became a cooperative rather than a real economic unity.

However, the fashion for progress at any cost, which marked the first stage and took its most symptomatic form in the conversion to Protestantism, started to ebb. Protestant missionaries asked their converts not to drink or smoke, and to abandon their domestic altars and family saints. They forbade them to dance the *jirana* which was the highest expression of collective joy and community solidarity—a solidarity which needed to be maintained in competition with other villages. This was too much to ask, and Chan Kom returned to Catholicism. But this was only one aspect of a general return to a more traditional style of life once the first fever of progress had abated.

Perhaps this return was also facilitated by the arrival of foreign families (in Redfield's day, one-third of the population of Chan Kom was made up of newly-arrived families) who could not integrate themselves except as Maya. And this in turn pushed the elders to return to a Mayan life-style to attract these newcomers to them. Redfield notes the following toward the end of his book: no formation of social classes; no creation of voluntary associations except for local and short-term projects; the tendency toward nucleation of families restrained by the preponderance of large families forming neighbourhood groups; side by side with political innovations like the municipal council, continuation of traditional religious organisation with its directors, choristers and sacristans and its systems of honourific roles.

'In the relations the inhabitants of Chan Kom have with one another' says Redfield, 'there are no great changes; it is still a community . . . All, young and old, see themselves as Indians, a people belonging to the forest, to the *milpa* and the village.' There is nothing, even going back to pre-Colombian paganism, which does not subsist: shamans are still present, holding rain-making ceremonies (even though the young attend these ceremonies more from fidelity to tradition than faith in the virtue of these rites; despite the building of stone houses, which limits the activities of the shaman, who used to perform rituals for laying the foundations of mud houses, but has no power over stone, cement or brick).

In fact, the balance-sheet which seems negative on many points actually shows only the slowness of the processes of acculturation, not their failure. Despite the variation of fashion and the ebb and flow of 'progressive' ideas, elements of change continue to act. A 'point of no return' is reached. If marriages are still arranged, the young have more and more say in the choice of partners; if women still prefer to live in their houses, they go out more often than before, and become accustomed to freedom of movement.

As Redfield puts it, cultural changes are not so impressive as social ones; because of the school the Indians now speak Spanish, the national language of Mexico, which is a factor in economic and political integration, while others who still speak indigenous dialects remain agents of marginalisation. Thus it is only possible to keep going ahead. Because Chan Kom chose this at the beginning of its evolution, it is now inexorably condemned to progress.

*   *   *

A certain number of conclusions for applied anthropology may be drawn from this general consideration of the laws of planned acculturation in the capitalist context, and from the two examples we have analysed. Once again, we leave aside the problem of ends. We do not wish to make value judgements about the ideology of economic and social progress. We state only, as an objective fact, that planned acculturation under a capitalist regime takes place under the sign of that ideology. The question that concerns us is thus to ascertain—given these ends—whether the means adopted to realise them are the best or not.

A first observation we can make is that—despite the integration of applied and general anthropology—both make use of the same concepts[6] which form strata of the same system: (a) empirical investigation, to describe the society as it is; (b) pure science, investigation of what it should become from what it is; (c) applied science, which is destined to push for a beginning of action by means of which the potentialities embodied in resources discovered by the empirical study are to be realised, and the obstacles which block their utilisation eliminated.[7] All the same, applied anthropology is, in this perspective, an 'applied art' and not a science.

Many who adopt a similar perspective would not be pleased by our conclusions. They reject the idea that the scholar should limit his activity to offering the materials of his research to the men of action, who will have the responsibility of applying these results as they see fit. They support an opposite position 'which considers knowledge not as an end in itself, but as an instrument of change or social reform . . . Investigation, in this case, is destined to offer a basis for social planning' and they affirm their conviction that 'investigation and action are only phases of the same polar process'.[8]

But who can fail to see that the integration of general and applied anthropology is only realised by raising action by one degree in the scale or system; that is, empirical investigation is already oriented, and not disinterested. It is selective and not theoretical or scientific. It is, in a word, a first stage of applied anthropology which will use in its empirical investigation the concepts and theories of general anthropology as it was constituted regardless of all practical application. Thus, from the beginning of the investigation, we are involved with 'art'; we have already left science as we understand it once the empirical research is oriented by what must be produced at the end.

The second observation we can make is that from this perspective, applied anthropology is concerned with the domain of social and cultural micro-organisms and not that of macro-organisms. This is one of the logical consequences of the evolution of general anthropology. After the failure of the great syntheses, like evolutionary theory or the historico-ethnological theory of culture circles, general anthropology is more and more oriented toward the study of small-scale 'communities', analysed in depth and in all their aspects—technological, economic, demographic, social, political, religious. The number of monographs has grown ceaselessly at the expense of universal theories.

And this means that when applied anthropology was formulated in America, it followed the then-current trend of pure anthropology and chose to try to change communities instead of changing the general organisation of the country. That is, it sought to work with the micro rather than with the macro. Fortifying this movement was the fact that the Indian had been defined not socially but culturally, in terms of his belonging to *isolated* communities, each different from the others, and of his costume, customs, etc., each tribe equally jealous of its own specificity.[9] Many probably retained a naive faith in the contagious force of reason which would mean that success in one of these communities would lead, through imitation, to a wish for change in the others and that this economic and social change would spread like an oil-slick, endlessly enlarging to cover the whole nation. Finally—and this should not be underestimated—the lack of sufficient capital and experts to act everywhere at once forced work with the Indians to be limited to local manipulations.

But North American cultural anthropology is in the process of transformation. It recognises that these communities are not in fact so isolated, that they participate to a greater or lesser extent in the culture of the global society, that they may well react. They are bound in a network of economic ties and are obliged to submit to political decisions taken outside, in the motor centres of the nation.

Briefly, the macroscopic point of view—which was long rejected by anthropology and relegated to sociology—has penetrated into anthropology which becomes regional and even national in scope rather than concerned with the understanding of a multitude of small communities. This is especially true following the remarks of J. H. Steward on 'the theory and practice of the study of culture areas'.[10] But does not applied anthropology risk dying as a proper science as a result of these remarks of Steward? Does it not run the risk of confusing itself with another science, which was born in parallel circumstances, and which took up macroscopy from its beginning, namely development sociology?

We shall take up this point when we try to define our own notion of applied anthropology as a science and not as a set of procedures for action. But in any case, the revolution in pure anthropology could not help having repercussions in the world of specialists in applied anthropology. We need no other evidence than that of the Mexican students at the last meeting of the Society for Applied Anthropology in April, 1969. They said,

'Social change has dynamics which are independent of change planned by the power structure. They have a specific sort of expression and manifest themselves in a whole series of movements whose sense is to concretise change, regardless of the consciousness the participants may have of it.

'The decay of institutions worries a sub-culture (here one means by a sub-culture one whose values are in conflict with the global culture) which finds itself unrepresented in these institutions, and which seeks their disappearance and their replacement by others which are better adapted. In this case, existing political structures, to represent the *status quo*, are traditionally opposed to change.

'However, it is this type of change which is dominant, and that is why anthropologists should apply themselves more conscientiously to it. In Mexico, the dominant type of anthropological material has been studies which show themselves to be conservative and anachronistic—studies of the community, with the community defined as an isolated reality which has its own dynamic.'

This quotation with its political undertones provides us with a suitable enough transition to the second form of planned acculturation that we must examine and criticise—planned acculturation in a socialist context.

NOTES

1. Cf. P. Ruopp, *Approaches to Community Development*, The Hague, Mouton, 1953; Margaret Mead (ed.), *Sociétés, traditions et technologie*, UNESCO, 1953; A. Caso, S. Zavala *et al.* *Metodos y resultados de la politica indigenista en Mexico*, Memorias del Inst. Nac. Indigen, VI, Mexico, 1954 etc.
2. On this point, cf. the recommendations of Condominas, *Fokon'Olona et collectivités rurales en Imérina*, Berger-Levrault, Paris, 1960.
3. G. Fisher, 'Directed Culture Change in Nayarit, Mexico', in *Synoptic Studies of Mexican Culture*.
4. On the nature of *ejidos*, see Caso, Zavala *et al*, op. cit.
5. R. Redfield, *A Village That Chose Progress: Chan Kom Revisited*, Phoenix Books, Chicago, 1948. Cf. R. Redfield, *The Folk Culture of Yucatan*, University of Chicago Press, Chicago, 1941.
6. For example, the concepts of status, role, organisation, process, etc., cf. R. N. Adams, *Introduccion a la Anthropologia Aplicada*, Seminario de Integracion Social, Guatemala, 1964.
7. G. A. Beltran, 'Teoria de la investigacion cultural', *Ciencias Sociales*, VII, 37, Washington, 1956.
8. G. A. Beltran, idem, pp. 23-4.
9. This conception seems to be abandoned today when it appears that the Indian can only define himself in relation to the *ladino*,

that is by the latter's policy of discrimination and segregation. This evolution appears clearly in the work of Beltran, which we discussed above: *Regiones de Refugio*, Mexico, 1967, as in the work of Stavenhagen, 'Clases, colonialismo y aculturacion', *Amer. Indigena*, 6, 1963. J. L. Herbert, 'Apuntes sobre la estructura nacional de Guatemala y el movimiento de ladinizacion', *Rev. Mex. de Sociol.*, XXXIX, 4, 1967; and in France, in the manuscript of thesis of Favre, *Changement et Continuité chez le Tzotzil-Tzeltal*.

10. J. H. Steward, *Area Research*, Social Science Research Council Bull., 63, New York, 1950.

While in the capitalist context it is first considered necessary to change micro-societies, planned acculturation in the socialist context works from top to bottom—from the structures of the global society down to local communities.

One may take exception to the former type in that it is content to adapt community cultures to that of the nation, that is to the culture of the dominant national minority. It is implied that this dominant culture is good, and that marginal groups must merely be integrated into it. The Mexican students' statement we quoted thus speaks correctly of the *status quo*. For if the Indians, thanks to nativist action, could be recovered, it was to a social structure which itself was not altered and thus to a class society where they occupied the lowest stratum.

If, on the contrary, planned acculturation begins at the top, it can cease to be a matter of imposition—that of the sub-culture of the dominant group on those of the dominated groups—and can take place in a revolutionary context. We do not claim that this will necessarily be the case. For each nation, everything depends on the decisions of political groups and on their power struggles. In any case, this is true as far as the USSR and her 'satellites' are concerned.

The first task of the Soviets was to break the hold of those in power, and to change the social organisation of the several global societies which were in their sphere of influence. Briefly—and here is the first difference between our two types of planned acculturation—the one is apolitical (or at least first appears to be so) while the other admits to being essentially political. This is the artefact of a transition from the micro to the macro. But further,

73

and taking the word 'democracy' in the Western sense, the former is democratic since it intends that the community itself take the decision for progress and engage itself collectively. The latter is non-democratic, and this is why people speak of Russian 'colonialism'. It is the imposition from without of a dictatorship—that said to be of the proletariat—which does not fear to use force to change global structures in order to permit, as a result, the transformation of national, regional or local cultures.

For example, it is known that in Kazakhstan, 30 per cent of the rural population had to move to Siberian industrial centres where manpower was lacking, and that the Kazakhs who remained preferred to slaughter their cattle rather than take them to collective farms where the Russians ordered them to live (27 per cent loss of horses, 17 per cent of large stock, and 19·5 per cent of sheep).

The second difference between our two types of acculturation is that they are implemented according to opposed strategies. The first desires initially to change cultures so that societies will change as a result. The second intially attacks the problem of social structure, believing that as a result, cultures will be modified of themselves. Certainly, this assertion must be qualified. The North American culturalists do try in their cautious and slow action to introduce changes in material techniques before trying to change mentalities and value systems. And the Soviets recognise the necessity of taking cultural facts into account. Stalin said cynically enough, 'the minorities aren't discontented about their loss of national independence, but rather about that of using their maternal languages'.

Lenin before him was always preoccupied not only with the modification of economic and social structures, but also with finding a process by which exotic cultures could be integrated with Russian culture which, in Russia, was both Western and proletarian; one which could take on wherever it spread congruous forms and means of expression suiting the peoples among whom it spread—a culture *sui generis* of general or universal value. 'Proletarian culture does not abolish national culture; it gives it content;

and, inversely, national culture does not abolish proletarian culture; it gives it form.'[1]

This statement does not take us far from planned acculturation in a capitalist context, where the latter attempts to adapt community cultures to that of the global society or, if one prefers, to the sub-culture of the group in power. Except that in the one case a capitalist sub-culture is in question while in the other it is a matter of a proletarian sub-culture. But even if, on the level of detail, there are qualifications to be made in our original assertion, it is nonetheless true that the ideologies that dictate the strategies whereby social realities are manipulated are opposed in these two differing contexts.

To understand planned acculturation in a socialist context, one must begin with Marx's distinction between structures and super-structures. Doubtless, there exists a dialectical relation in the evolution of societies between economic and extra-economic factors. Cultural factors in particular must be considered in a policy of development, since economic values—if they are taken on the one hand in the texture of social relations—on the other are correlated with cultural values. However, it is still economic factors, the forces and relations of production, which are, in the final analysis, preponderant: the means of production—that is, machines and primary materials—the relations of production—that is, the organisation of labour and the judicial relations which regulate the rights of men to these means, machines and primary materials. Modifications which intervene in the means of production, such as scientific and technical discoveries, cause parallel modifications in the relations of production which must correspond to them. And in its turn, the transformation of these relations acts on superstructures and thus, at the same time, on mentalities (attitudes, ideas and theories) and on institutions (judicial, political, religious) which are attached to them.

What is the logical consequence of all this for applied anthropology? It is that it is not necessary to affect language and ethnic cultures; instead, it is necessary to change first, if not uniquely, the system of production, and all the superstructures, which are linked to the old regime, will change in a parallel way. Or, if they continue to survive for a while through force of habit, they will only continue to survive as 'folklore', without real efficacy. Briefly then, American applied anthropology is 'cultural,' and Russian applied anthropology is 'sociological'.

But these two differences are not the only ones. Or, more exactly, they are closely linked to give rise to a third important strategic difference. For if development comes from outside, if this development must first break down the former structures of economic relations and create new ones; if the 'midwifely' force of the new societies is necessary for this; in a word, if primacy is given from the outset to the political and the economic, it is still true that the structural revolution can only succeed if one concentrates on certain sectors of the society that one wants to change as against others. That is, if one succeeds in introducing the class struggle as a means of intervention preliminary to change.

So there is certainly a common point in our two types of planned acculturation—the search for the leaders most likely to succeed in realising the desired transformations. But since the underlying ideologies are opposite, they will not search for them at the same level. Similarly, the role of these leaders in both cases is that of intermediaries, required to convert the exogenous into the endogenous, first themselves internalising the donor culture so as to spread it among the recipient group. But since the culture of the donor group is in the first case the national one, and in the second the proletarian one, the first sort of leaders will try for continuity. That is, they are chosen as those in the community who will be most capable of providing a syncretism of new ideas and traditional customs, or of reinterpreting the former. The second sort of leaders will seek discontinuity. That is, they are chosen among those who can best become conscious of their exploitation by a privileged minority, and become leaders of a revolutionary movement.

As we have said, in planned acculturation within the capitalist system, the leaders who are called on are usually heads of villages, elders, and the most experienced members of the community—

the best-loved who may thus have an influence since they have the confidence of all. In planned acculturation in the socialist system, leaders are not those designated by the organisation of the community. They must be sought out—and to discover them, one must progress through the class struggle, for it is only in that struggle and by means of it that the oppressed can become conscious of their situation of oppression, and therefore desire to change the old forms. Further, within that struggle, an automatic selection occurs by which leaders emerge from the group of followers. Finally, we must add that in these conditions, it is likely that the leaders who would be chosen in the capitalist context become in the socialist one 'the men to pull down'. The inversion is total.

In any case, it seems that almost everywhere in the satellite Soviet Republics, change began with the class struggle and the destruction of the old political and economic forms. In Kirghizia, this occurred between the Bolshevik Party, the large agricultural owners, and the urban bourgeoisie. Here, to realise the creation of new economic structures of production this had to be preceded by changing the local leaders and destroying the local, feudal political structure.

In Mongolia, where the peasant masses, oppressed by the Manchu Dynasty, had revolted several times in the second half of the nineteenth century, and finally appealed to the Russians in 1921, it was also necessary through the instruments of the class struggle to proceed at the same time against the military-feudal bureaucracy of the Chinese, against the Lamas—considered as the offspring of the old class of feudal masters, whose church was also considered by the Russians to be a veritably feudal institution—and against the class of commercial capitalists. This struggle was not waged without losses: to break the hold of the feudal masters, the collectives were multiplied; to break the hold of the priests, cloisters were liquidated; the Lamas were made to do manual labour, and the education of the young was taken out of their hands. But it was in these struggles that leaders were forged, on whom the Russians could then rely in their policies of social and economic change.

If American applied anthropology recognises that there are no societies without internal tensions, and if it takes the greatest possible advantage of these conflicts of interest in order to progress toward modern ends for the entire collectivity, it nonetheless considers that:

(1) The centripetal forces of cohesion are stronger than the centrifugal forces of dissolution. All cultures constitute systems of equilibrium between counter-balancing forces, which complement each other naturally.

(2) Society is part of culture, that is relations between men and groups are regulated by the norms, values and ideas of culture.

(3) Progress should occur at the least cost and for the benefit of all.

We now see that Soviet applied anthropology considers on the contrary that:

(1) All non-socialist societies are full of internal contradictions, and if these contradictions do not lead to a change of regime, it is because of the constraints laid on the masses by the privileged minority group and not because of some sort of organic resistance to culture, to the forces of dissolution which it, itself, contains.

(2) Culture is properly speaking more a part of the social super-structure than of its structure.

(3) Progress is costly; it cannot be other than costly, since the forces that prevent it must be broken. It is obvious that it cannot benefit all, since the interests of the privileged cannot be identified with the interests of those they exploit for their personal profit.

Thus, American applied anthropology stresses the unity of culture and its homogeneity at the expense of recognising social stratification and conflict. Soviet applied anthropology stresses social conflict and the class struggle at the expense of recognising the fact that all classes share at least a certain number of common values. This is because behind these two strategies of economic and social development there is on the one hand a relativist cultural anthropology and, on the other, an anthropology faithful to the evolutionism of Morgan.

Morgan maintained that all societies pass sooner or later through the same stages of development, knowing at a given moment the same internal contradictions, and that these contradictions, when they become insupportable, are the origin—together with the discovery of new means of production—of structural change and human progress. Thus, lineal, feudal or tribal societies, when exposed to Russian propaganda, will proceed of themselves to a superior stage of development. What anthropology shows then is that if they did not do it before, it is because they were arrested in their evolution by conservative forces which profited from their stagnation, and which kept them from progressing because such progress would lead to the end of the privileges of those forces. The Russians are thus merely the accelerators of history; but they can accelerate it only if they obey it. That is, they must respect the law Marx revealed: that socialism can only be born in the class struggle. Thus, the two great themes of Marxism— historical determinism and the apology of *praxis*—are joined. And the adversaries of Marxism sometimes oppose them erroneously.

The Americans and the Russians agree on one point, namely that it is necessary to begin with social totalities. But then they are in disagreement about the choice of these totalities. The cultural anthropologists tend to think of partial totalities—communities or regions—while the Marxists, since they are evolutionists, tend to think of the present total society. 'The attitude that consists in seeking the causes and, even more, the remedies of our ills in the social structure of a so-called "isolated" community', they say, 'or only in a so-called "national" society, or in the third of the world that Wendel Wilkie had already defined as forming a whole, is a method which is empirically false, theoretically inadequate, and practically absurd.'[2] For the Third World is only understood and defined by the developed countries, nations by their places in a system of world-wide imperialism, and communities by their relation to the constraints of national governments.

Secondly, they both have a different notion of these totalities, the former a functionalist one and the latter, a dialectical one. So, 'there is a great difference between the notions functionalism and dialecticism develop à propos the totality. The functionalists . . . speak of the totality only to discern the part. But concerning the totality itself, they scarcely trouble themselves; they do not ask why it exists, what its origins are, or what its future may be; they do not pose the question whether it is acceptable as it is or not, they accept willingly the global system as it is, and take as ready money the social structure as they find it. At best, they try to understand it, and perhaps reform a part. For the Marxists on the other hand, the condition *sine qua non* of science is first precisely to analyze and to explain the origin, nature and development of the social system in its entirety, and its structure as a whole, and then to employ the understanding thus achieved as a necessary base for the analysis and understanding of its parts.'[3]

That is to say, to the opposition microscopy–macroscopy is added another; Marxist anthropology is historical and not cultural. It becomes clearer then why these two theoretical conceptions give rise to such different sorts of applied anthropology. The first, cultural anthropology, would transform the whole, starting with its constituent elements. The second, Marxist anthropology, does not seek to transform the particular first, since the particular is determined by the general. Instead, it attacks the socio–economic structure of the whole, because that determines the parts. And this is especially true as regards culture since, as we have seen, culture is viewed as essentially a superstructure, not a structure.

*   *   *

Even though the guiding principles of these two types of planned acculturation are so opposite, and the corresponding strategies of development that arise from them are so different, one sees that in terms of the facts of change, as these emerge, there is no great difference. Nor can there be. For with principles we remain in the realm of ideology, while facts obey laws which science must discover. Regardless of the action of men, whether it starts at one point or another—from the isolated community or the whole of humanity—'one conquers nature only by obeying her'. If not, nature rebels against man.

Despite the distinction made between the human and the natural sciences—and though the principle of recurrence may be exact and we become what we believe we are, or that social facts end up by remodelling themselves after the notion we have of them—social determinism does exist, as studies of acculturation have shown. And this is all the more true in that no matter what conception of applied anthropology is used, exactly the same laws are found in one case as in the other, and without the social laws being modified in either their content or form by the ideological principles that may guide the given action. Man is neither a thaumaturge nor a god. And his prime quality—which he tends to forget today—should be modesty. There are laws, and they must be obeyed once they have been discovered. Reality can only be transformed if they are observed and not if they are ignored.

These laws or regularities that we have enumerated à propos free acculturation are accepted by planned acculturation in the capitalist context and made the best of. We shall now see that they apply to planned acculturation in the socialist context, though this is certainly not expected.

First let us take that of reinterpretation. When a culture trait is borrowed or imposed from outside by a cultural or social system, the form may remain unchanged but the trait is reinterpreted in terms of the old system, which gives it a new meaning, different from the one it had in the donor system. We saw that planned acculturation in the capitalist context started from this very assumption, and sought leaders of change among those in the recipient society who were most apt at finding reinterpretations that would lead to ready acceptance.

The distain Russian anthropologists display for those American studies that have a bearing on acculturative processes has made them neglect, to their cost, this essential aspect of all acculturation. The Russian imposed *kolkhoses* and *sovkhoses* in the Central

Asian Republics, but the old social structures that they believed were destroyed re-emerged within the newly-imposed forms. Collective enterprises came to be organised in terms of lineages, giving rise to stunted collectives of ten to twenty holdings whose productivity was insufficient. Later, in a more authoritarian phase, these dwarf *kolkhoses* were replaced by an institution modelled on the Russian type. Still, several ethnic groups were forced to live together, retaining their own holdings, and their reciprocal hostility which more than ever decreased their productivity.[4]

These resistances of local or national cultures to any change that might destroy them—if the change is not adopted by the culture—are exemplified by the position of women. The Soviets, knowing that sociologically women are generally less likely than men to accept innovation (there are exceptions, particularly in urban Africa) wished to eliminate the woman as guardian of tradition by enacting a whole series of laws concerning the veil, marriage of pre-pubescent girls, polygamy and the levirate.

They presented such legislation as a class struggle or, alternatively, they declared that they did not wish to alter the traditional relation of inequality between the sexes, but only to help women to become instruments in the building of socialism, which required the work of all. But regardless of these campaigns, even wives of Party members wear the veil; precocious marriage, marriage by capture, the ransoming of brides, and polygamy continue, while tying to reinterpret themselves in Soviet terms. It is still difficult to get women to vote, to work in factories, and to mix with men at receptions.

This is because Islam was seen as a superstructure which would modify itself as the relations of production changed. Culture was no longer taken as a universality since in Marxism the globality is on a more general level. The task then consisted in neutralising the mosques and transforming them into clubs or shops; in nationalising unalienable wealth, and making the Muslim faith a private matter and not a central element or the cultural focus. Or in transforming the main religious festivals—such as the sacrifice—by forbidding the slaughter of sheep for ritual purposes—or the breaking of the fast into purely domestic and quasi-clandestine rituals, while the rhythm of factory work made the five daily prayers impossible.

All observers agree that despite these efforts, Islam in the Muslim Soviet republics is thriving. And this validates cultural anthropological theory which maintains that culture forms a system and not a simple superstructure translating the forces and relations of production into ideas.[5] Still, atheist propaganda is spreading more and more and thus we discover another law in action—one of the fundamental laws of religious acculturation. That is, that a religion under attack from without does not disappear but transforms itself either into magic or into secret brotherhood cults.[6] In the case under discussion, the diminution of persecuted Muslim Orthodoxy was accompanied by a falling back on popular forms of religion (the cult of Saints persists) or a resurgence of pre-Islamic cults—formerly suppressed and subsisting only among women—once the control of Orthodoxy was broken.[7]

Soviet planned acculturation did not change to forced acculturation with impunity. (Yet this change has frequently caused talk in the West about Russian 'colonialism'.) This change was due to a voluntary misunderstanding of the laws or regularities of the acculturative process. In a word, a misunderstanding of the existence of a determinism that curbs *praxis* and that *praxis* must respect in order to succeed.

But forced acculturation also obeys laws or regularities, as we have seen. The displacement or deporting of the indigenous populations from the Muslim areas, e.g., the Volga and the Caucasus, to Siberia and the replacement of them with Russian colonists had certain affects which are exactly the same as in the case of capitalist colonisation. A new system of social stratification succeeded the old; it placed the Russian cadres at the top in the administration of factories, and the indigenous sweepers, gardeners and porters at the bottom. There was a reclassification of individuals that allowed 'évolués' to rise in the society—though under the direct control of the Communist Party, and the indirect control of the Russians—while the transplanted Russians divided themselves into middle and upper groups on the one hand, and 'poor whites' on the other.

From this ensued—on the part of the poor whites especially—an intensification of racial or ethnic prejudices, and the development of a 'superiority complex' on the part of the Russians which in turn led to endogamous marriages, and separation of the ethnicities in contact. Russian and Uzbek workers did not mix outside the factory gates. Their children played separately at school. And this separation was manifested not only in life-style—each ethnicity retaining its own customs—but also by an equally different standard of living (from which arose inter-ethnic tensions which, since they could not be manifested openly, were transformed into poetic glorification of the national heroes of long ago).[8] Thus a whole series of facts which were characteristic of colonisation and, before that, of slavery, are found here again, *mutatis mutandis*, to the extent that planned acculturation, being unable to change the laws of social determinism, is brought to a standstill if it does not admit its failure and becomes forced acculturation.

*　*　*

The reader who remembers the first part of this chapter will understand the origins of this failure. They lie in the fact that at another level, the progress of archaic or feudal societies to the most modern industrialisation is seen as an undeniable success which is proven by all the statistics. The Russians started with an evolutionist anthropology and we know that evolutionary theory never paid much attention to phenomena of contact—borrowing, exogenous modification—and emphasised only developmental sequences. And even before Marx, it emphasised 'subsistence arts' which can be called means of production, and institutions like the family, types of ownership, or types of political organisation which we may call the relations of production.

And this causes Soviet applied anthropology to be confused with what is now called development sociology. It will suffice here to show that, for the Russians, these two sciences, and the applied arts that follow from them, tend to become mixed.

Only in the case we have been considering—that of the satellite Soviet Republics—industrialisation and its golden rule, namely the continuous increase of productivity, is introduced from outside, that is from Russia which has become an industrialised country, into other countries which had remained pre-industrial and which all have their specific cultures. And this means that their 'development' or progress from a pre-industrial to an advanced industrial level—at which even agriculture is industrialised and commercialised—could only occur in terms of acculturation.

In this chapter, we wished to make a point about planned acculturation. We have found that:

(1) We must distinguish two aspects—development, which follows certain laws, and acculturation, which also follows certain regularities.

(2) When a policy of development is introduced from without, and is expressed through culture contact, the laws of development must take account of those of acculturation.

The error of American applied anthropology, at least until the last two decades, was to make more of the latter than of the former. And the error of Soviet applied anthropology was to emphasise the former over the latter. Be this as it may, what is important for us is that we have shown that there exists a social determinism, and that because of this, applied anthropology in order to be effective must be based on this realisation. It must be accepted if applied anthropology wants to find the best means for instituting its goals which are, in fact, value judgements.

Before going further, we must discuss in more detail the choice of leaders—a question which has arisen twice in the last chapters. Having elucidated the ends and the means of planning, we must turn to its instruments.

NOTES

1. Stalin, *Marxism and the National and Colonial Question*, Lawrence & Wishart, London, 1942.
2. A. Gunder Frank, 'Fonctionalisme et dialectique', *L'Homme et la Société*, 12, Paris, 1969, p. 143.
3. Idem, p. 142.
4. *Soviet Central Asia*, Human Relations Area Files, New Haven, 3 vols.
5. V. Monteil, *Les Musulmans Soviétiques*, Ed. du Seuil, Paris, 1957.
6. R. Bastide, *Éléments de Sociologie Réligieuse*, 1st ed., A. Colin, Paris, 1935.
7. S. P. and E. Dunn, 'Soviet Regime and Native Culture in Central Asia and Kazakhstan', *Current Anthropology* VIII, 3, 1967.
8. V. Monteil, op. cit.

Defence and Illustration of Marginality

1 Luso-Tropocology

Is it proper in considering contacts between different civilisations only to study the reactions of the recipient civilisation when confronted by the donor? Basically, studies of acculturation, whether free, forced or planned, remain ethnocentric precisely to the extent that they are concerned with the impact of a so-called 'superior' culture on another that it modifies, and with the analysis of what transpires in the latter while the characteristics of the carrier-culture are left aside. True, cultural anthropologists did formulate the following rule: one must study the transformations that occur in both cultures, not only in one of them.[1] René Maunier, in his *Sociologie Coloniale*, devotes several pages to the change undergone by colonisers in the tropics, by those who accept the indigenous life-style, marry local women, and unconsciously allow themselves to be invaded by the culture of their surrounding milieu.[2]

But though cultural anthropology provides a complete inventory of problems for study, ethnologists make choices from it, and certain items are neglected. Among these, transformations of Western culture under the influence of exotic cultures is one that has evoked the least interest. Even though Maunier took up this question, he only saw it in terms of the first stage of colonisation, the pioneer phase when whites left without their families, when they were very few, and in a sense were drowned in the indigenous mass. And the terminology that he uses to express these phenomena, e.g., the 'indigenisation' of Westerners, is indicative of negative value judgements, and a condemnation of the phenomenon of 'marginalisation'.

But does this marginalisation of whites in contact with Indians,

Africans or Asians correspond only to the first stage of colonisation? Can it not be an enrichment of one culture by another, rather than a policy of abandon, of descent into the abyss, or a desertion of the 'white man's burden' and its implied responsibilities, especially since no culture has absolute superiority? What determines the attitude of individuals in Diaspora is ultimately dependent on the ethnic cultures to which they belong.

In the preceding chapters, we have left aside the whole question of differences among the various Western ethnicities. We have spoken of our own European civilisation acting on exotic cultures as though it had a separate existence, instead of being incarnated in various ethnic cultures each with its own value system and behavioural norms. What Gilberto Freyre called 'Luso-tropocology' is a political ideology as well as a 'science'. But still, it is part of science and we shall analyse it here as such, leaving aside the implications it may have for the maintenance of Portuguese colonialism. One proof of the scientific usefulness of this theory was its acceptance in various European universities—especially in England, whose institutes were interested in the effects of the tropics on whites and their own cultures. It further shows that though this theory also served as an apology for Portugal, it was something more as well.[3]

Freyre says that the Portuguese—and, to a lesser degree, the Spanish—showed an awareness of the techniques, methods and values of tropical peoples. They adopted their systems of building, diet, more relaxed habits, methods of hygiene, and empirical medicine. So Maunier is probably right. At the beginning of the fifteenth century, Europeans coming from the Iberian Peninsula and elsewhere, suffered a semi-dissolution of their 'European-ness' under the influence of non-European styles of living, imposed by the tropical climate and intimate mixing with the local population.

But what is new is that, even when the proportion of colonists rose, they still did not impose their own, European, life-style. Instead, they created a 'symbiotic culture, composed of the European heritage as adapted to the tropical environment, and enriched by tropical experience'. Freyre speaks almost poetically of 'Europeans resident or situated in the tropics, integrated into a new time-space, linked to tropical cultures, nourishing themselves with tropical plants and animals, treated or cured of tropical diseases with tropical remedies', wearing cotton instead of wool, sleeping in hammocks instead of stifling in beds. And he defines the adaptation of these men to their new ecological milieu as a 'voluptuous' one.

The black slave trade and the development of slavery changed this political situation only by the introduction of black 'mammies' and 'coloured lovers'. The Portuguese—who in America had already incorporated so many Indian culture traits into their half-caste culture—thus also incorporated African traits as well: tales, recipes, curative techniques, animist religious beliefs, etc.[4] And this they also did 'voluptuously', by raising their children with the help of attentive black women, to whom the children remained linked biologically, and introducing them to sex through the intermediary of some half-caste woman or coloured serving girl, a bit of whose polytheist soul they received along with their bodies.

In this chapter we must emphasise this sexual component of the adaptation—and not the imposition—of European culture to the exigencies of life in the tropics. The Portuguese re-created themselves everywhere in innumerable half-caste children, which meant that:

(1) A tiny country was able to populate a vast colonial empire; the Portuguese conquered the world not with the cross or the sword, but with sexuality, proliferating themselves in Euro-Amerindians, Euro-Asians, and Euro-Africans.

(2) This hybridisation formed a protective covering that kept the gears from sticking in the meshing of one culture with another.

(3) The half-castes eventually served as intermediaries in the transmission of Western values, or at least those seen as adaptable to the tropics, to the indigenous mass, and they constituted, so to speak, indispensable transmission relays in the acculturative process, so that those values would be accepted.

Thus the Portuguese discovered as pioneers what anthropologists are only now discovering, namely the importance of 'mixed-bloods' or 'marginals' as leaders of change and as principals responsible for community development. For the moment, we need only state that the processes of acculturation vary not only in relation to the so-called 'recipient' ethnicities, but also with the characteristics of the so-called 'donor' ethnicities—given that, in these cultural marriages, each one is simultaneously both donor and recipient.

Naturally, one asks what motivated the Portuguese, and to a certain extent the Spanish, to adapt their Luso-Hispanic civilisations to the indigenous tropical civilisations rather than setting them above, in all their immutability. One may think of historical causes. The Spanish, and even more the Portuguese, having been conquered by the Moors, were thus already somewhat 'Africanised' or 'tropicalised' before their colonial experience. They had already acquired through this preliminary miscegenation with Moors and Muslims the voluptuous sentiment of exoticism, the propensity to receive as much as to give.

One also thinks of the preponderant influence of Catholicism in Latin cultures.[5] For the central dogma of Catholicism is that of incarnation—the new Spirit incarnates itself in the body to change it from within, and the body in the case of collectivities is their civilisation. This is opposed to the central dogma of Protestantism, namely Crucifixion, which holds that the old Adam should be destroyed, so that the new Adam may be born. That is, in the case of collectivities, that the old civilisations must be entirely destroyed, crucified, so that a new Christian civilisation may be born; 'you can't put new wine in old bottles'. Certainly, the nature of religious belief plays an important role, as we shall show by comparing these Latin ethnicities to other ethnicities that have transmitted civilisation, namely the Anglo-Saxons and the Slavs.

As opposed to this adaptation and acceptance of what foreign cultures have that is good or savoury, for the so-called 'conquering' culture—which thus allows itself to be conquered as it conquers—Anglo-Saxon acculturation seems eager to distinguish clearly between the donor group, which has nothing to receive, and the recipient group. The latter is seen as the only one that must change, adapt, and be transformed so as to adapt more fully. True, it too knew a stage of miscegenation—the existence of half-castes in the United States and the Republic of South Africa is the proof. But these half-castes were relegated more and more to the category 'negroes' instead of being recognised as indispensable partners in the exchanges or reinterpretations of differing civilisations. (In the US, many of the half-castes were created by the French occupation of Louisiana. In the Cape Colony, they were the result of passing affairs of soldiers or sailors and not the product of a union between the Dutch and Africans.)

Union with natives always seemed a form of prostitution, or a sacrilege to these good Puritans. The sensuality of the woman of colour, be she Indian or African—a sensuality that religious censure rendered even greater at the imaginary level than it was in reality —seemed only a temptation to sin held out by the Devil to the sons of God. Far from encouraging individual miscegenation, which would have led to the marriage of cultures, Anglo-Saxon civilisation hardened itself through separation and segregation, already raising the first 'wall of shame' between co-existing ethnicities. As opposed to the relations of reciprocity, amalgamation, and formation of mixed cultures seen in the countries colonised by the Latins, here we find relations of non-integration, exteriorisation of the so-called donor culture vis-à-vis others, and the acceptance of syncretism or marginality only if they occurred in the so-called recipient culture.

Protestantism—especially the Calvinist and sectarian varieties— gave the Anglo-Saxons the feeling that they, and they alone, were in the right and, consequently, that their culture was the only valid one. True, insofar as their ethnic culture was mixed with religion, they did not push away native cultures with disdain. Rather, they pitied the natives for not yet having known the light of the True Faith. At first, the Puritans treated the Indians as brothers, to whom they must bring the benefits of God's Word, and the merits of their own uniquely valid civilisation.

But the Indians refused; they retained, even in their Christianity, whole sections of their traditional 'superstitions'. They borrowed certain European culture traits which they reinterpreted in terms of their own value systems. By a *quid pro quo* that was tragic for themselves, they even seemed to turn backward, since they sold their land to the first whites who arrived on their shores. But they did not have the same notions of contract as the whites. They had not, as the Puritans believed, sold the ownership of the land—which for them was inalienable—but only the usufruct. When they asked for it back, they were seen as incapable of keeping promises, or as driven by Satan.[6]

And so a Manichean notion of culture conflict was born in which on one side was the Right, and on the other, the Diabolical. Later, from the eighteenth century on, this opposition became secularised. But it was to remain and leave its mark on theories of acculturation. In this way, we see that the end result of Luso-tropocology is reciprocal adaptation and fusion, thanks to a dual change of both cultures. But the end result in Anglo-Saxon cultural anthropology is a linear process which must result in the assimilation of the natives to Western culture.

Analagous observations may be made about the Slavs. It is not for nothing that the Chinese accuse the Russians of continuing the imperialist policies of the Czars of all the Russias. Here again, politics is penetrated by religion, or is rather the current secularisation of a great mystical dream, that of the Slavic people seen as the continuation of Christ, and called upon by a special grace to save the world by regenerating it. The transition from Czarism to Communism merely changed the content of this faith, but not the idea that Russia has a universalistic mission to fulfil, for the good of all men. Unconsciously, the dream of the Holy Orthodox Church still animates the builders of dams and the creators of great industrial complexes in the Asian steppes. Marxism, from being a sociological science, becomes an ethnic ideal of thaumaturgic *praxis*, that accepts only with difficulty the idea that other countries can save themselves by discovering their own original roads for the march toward socialism.

So, we see that the very conceptions that anthropologists have of acculturation, of its goals and paths, depend not only on the empirical investigations they can carry out, but also on the acculturative situations in which they work—and that these situations in turn are the heritage of the ethnic notions of their predecessors. In the same way, we can imagine the elaboration of a whole 'ethnology' of knowledge that would complete the sociology of knowledge, and might even constitute a chapter thereof, since it involves the matter of the influence of groups on scientific research—here the group being the global society and not one of its sectors, e.g., one social class or another. But it will differ from the latter, since the sociology of knowledge seeks to ascertain the effects of the scholar's position in a certain structure of human relations and of the interests linked to that position. An ethnology of knowledge would only be concerned with values and ideas, cultural habits or attitudes, imposing themselves from without on the researcher belonging to that ethnicity.

But we do not wish to lead the reader in this direction. We wish only to show the existence of another form of acculturation, that to which Freyre gave the name 'Luso-tropocology' and which is achieved by a justification of the double integration or amalgamation of so-called 'marginal' cultures with respect both to Western and to indigenous cultures. This form exists aside from the two types of planned acculturation which, despite their opposition, agree in restricting change to exotic cultures, considered either implicitly or explicitly as 'backward' or 'underdeveloped'.

This defence and illustration of marginality—not in terms of mixed collective cultures, but of the preponderant role of marginal individuals in community development—is being rediscovered today by North American applied anthropology. We may now take up the thread of our discourse again, and examine the human factors in this acculturation.

11 *Leaders of the Acculturative Gambit*

We have established that acculturation cannot succeed except in so far as it arouses the enthusiasm, or at least the adherence, of the recipient group. We have also seen that a schism may occur in the recipient group, one faction accepting change and the other refusing it. For example, during the colonial era there was the rupture between the 'évolués' and the peasant masses. Or in a stratified society, that between the new class of large landowners who will accept innovation and the plebians who do not wish to change their attitudes. In these cases, at least in the short term, acculturation has only partially succeeded, since two societies were created where there had only been one. We need only remember the many examples of 'dualism' in the countries of Latin America, divided as they are between progressive elites and the traditional masses.

The choice of leaders is thus important for an acculturation to be globally successful, as it should be. We have seen, finally, that there are two different attitudes toward the choice of these leaders, which are characteristic of our two types of planned acculturation. The Europeans choose individuals who, because of their social status, their age or their experience, have more prestige and power, with the idea that the mass will follow them. (Thus, missionaries at first tried to convert chiefs since the conversion of chiefs almost automatically led to that of their followers.)

The Soviets, on the contrary, concentrate on the disinherited, dominated and exploited strata, to incite them to revolutionary combat and to changes via the class struggle that follows. And from this struggle emerge the leaders who will be capable of leading their societies toward economic progress, forging it and finally imposing it. If, in this second case, we come near to the question of marginals, we are still far from the end, since the marginality of the oppressed is seen as a structural rather than a cultural one.

It appears that during the birth of applied anthropology, no one thought to utilise the cultural marginals as leaders of the acculturative gambit. This is because the cultural anthropology on which it was based, took a pessimistic view of marginality.[7] The marginal man was he who participates in two different cultures, which are in conflict within him, so that he feels divided. He may be a half-caste, but there is also cultural hybridisation which is independent of miscegenation.

True, it was recognised that these marginal people were more intelligent than others, that they might have a sharper and more critical mentality. Nevertheless, the old cultural anthropology emphasised the factor of split personality, which was expressed in fluctuating and contradictory actions, or in permanently ambivalent attitudes. Secondly, it emphasised the compensatory reactions by means of which the marginal man tried to overcome his internal conflicts—e.g., inferiority-superiority complex, hypersensitivity, paranoic-type defence mechanisms. Thirdly, it emphasised the maladjustment of such individuals, rejected simultaneously by both societies to which they belonged. Being unable to integrate themselves into either, marginal men ended by becoming neurotic, frustrated and embittered. They made up the highest statistical proportion of suicides and of the mentally ill.

True, it was also recognised that this internal conflict could not go on indefinitely—that it had to be resolved. The marginal man must finally become assimilated to one culture or another. But if he became assimilated to the culture of the minority group, he would feel that he had forfeited something, and so this was not a real solution. And if he was assimilated to the majority group culture, he would feel that he was in some way betraying his ancestors, and would become even more confused. As a result, his victory over this conflict would amount to a still more bitter defeat.

This is a legitimate picture of the marginal man, but it does not seem to conform to the marginal man in racist societies. Here, personality disorganisation seems more the effect of discrimination and segregation than of the existence of two selves in conflict. Or, if you will, we are attempting here an analysis of the psychological consequences of structural rather than cultural marginality.

Contemporary anthropology, taking account of sociological situations, brings to light other solutions once we leave aside racist societies. We have shown elsewhere, for example, that the men of the *candomblés* of Brazil live without difficulty in two different worlds—that of Africanist brotherhoods for their religious activities and that of Brazilian political associations, unions etc., for their technological, economic and social activities.[8] Balandier shows in the same way that when the African finds himself in his fields, he continues to follow the animist tradition, and that in the village square—once he is touched by urban civilisation—he changes his attitudes and mentality so as to live in the modern world.[9]

North American sociology now tends to substitute the distinction between action groups and reference groups for the portrayal of the marginal man. Both of the former can sometimes be the same (e.g. the Mexicans in the Southern United States can both be and feel Mexican) they may also be distinct (here, the action group would be Mexican but the reference group would be the Anglo-Saxon one). Thus, this simultaneous integration into two cultures, far from being considered as marginality, is seen by sociologists as a normal evolution and a progression by progressive internalisation of the values, ideas and norms seen as superior.[10] Finally, we must distinguish between marginal individuals and marginal groups. If a marginal individual lives in a marginal group, he is well adapted, and the one who will not be adapted will be the non-marginal man who belongs to only one culture.

Williams gives a good example of this, that of Teuto-Brazilians. These people, while retaining their Germanic heritage as regards their language, religion, certain folkloric traditions and a particular notion of the family, are at the same time 'cablocised' by taking up part of the culture of the Brazilian peasant. In this syncretist society, it is when a new German immigrant arrives—carrying with him the integrity of German culture—that he himself will feel 'maladjusted,' 'outside,' or 'foreign' precisely because he has not yet become marginal.[11]

We see then that from a first negative portrayal of marginality, we have passed little by little, under pressure from the facts, to one that is more positive. Here writers were ahead of scholars. For while anthropologists were still moulding their notion of the traumatised and neurotic marginal man; in France André Gide, in his famous polemic against Maurice Barrès, wrote a defence of uprootedness as an indispensable basis for the triumph of individual freedom and for creative originality.

Empirical anthropological research not only changed the old notion of the marginal man. It also suggested that he could play a definitive role in community development. This would logically be true if:

(1) The contradiction between values that leads to economic change on the one hand, and characteristics of a general culturally-determined wind of change on the other, became so insufferable that the community could only resolve it by creating new behavioural norms and;

(2) the marginal man could not resolve his previous conflicts, and since he could not change himself as actor in two cultures, he would change the milieu he lived in. Since he could not adapt himself to it, he would have to adapt it to suit himself. He would transform his group into a marginal group in which he would then be well-adjusted.

So it was concluded that, at least theoretically, the only leader who could facilitate a transition from tension to re-equilibration must be chosen from among marginal men, or even from among 'neurotics'. More than the prestigious chief, it would be the eccentric who would be the best animator and manipulator of the community. In the last chapter, we saw that Chan Kom chose progress because it had first been formed as a village by young secessionist Indians who were in revolt against the power of their elders.

Organisers of economic and social planning have occasionally instituted preliminary investigations of the leadership structure of the communities they hoped to deal with. Here we shall give only one such example. In choosing it we hope to show that our conclusions are all the more valid since it is taken from a non-Indian village community in a developing and not an underdeveloped country, namely Argentina.[12] This investigation, carried out at Pocito in the State of San Juan, showed the following:

(1) If we take the raw figures, the most renowned of the leaders of this community was named 56 times, which means that he had

great influence over about 12 per cent of the population. This percentage would have been sufficient to lead to a change in attitudes and behaviour in the direction of progress if this leader had been chosen by the planning commission. But such a choice would mean little in itself, since the social class, standard of living, etc. of those who chose him must be taken into account, as well as the type of objectives of the influence he exercised.

(2) It appeared that the leaders of the community—those who had the highest prestige and who were listened to—were recruited from the highest strata of the population: 87·8 per cent were independent professionals; 71·6 per cent were landowners; neither peons, farmers nor workers chose their leaders from their own social categories. Peasants chose industrialists or professionals from the provincial capital.

(3) These leaders could be classed according to two types—traditional and progressive. The investigation shows that 38·4 per cent of leaders, before taking decisions, consulted their relatives, neighbours, or friends as is characteristic of traditional societies. Only 12·6 per cent of the leaders read or listened to the technical information available in papers and on the radio concerning the way to cause a community to progress. The investigating body in charge of planning for the region was little known. It was known that in San Juan, the capital, there were experts in agriculture, sanitation, etc., but none of these experts was named as leader. They were all perceived as not belonging to the community, as strangers to it; and as we know, peasants take a dim view of strangers.

If one questions these peasants, one finds that the advice they ask of those they recognise as leaders refers to small daily problems of life—problems of farming or work, personal or family problems—and not problems relevant to the technical progress of the community. In sum, the vast majority of influential persons in the area, then, belong to the group of traditional leaders and not to that of progressive ones.

(4) One must go further. Since these leaders belong to the most privileged class, and since in this community prestige is tied to

economic power, there is a social distance between them and the mass of the population such that these leaders merely defend their class interests, and their influence can only be exerted in favour of the *status quo*. The progress they accept can only be progress 'for them' as a class with relatively high status, and not progress for all. All agrarian reform, for example, would be fought against by them, and they would make use of all their prestige to avert it. We thus validate our previous conclusion, namely that progress cannot come from the more or less prestigious leaders of the community. Its leaders must be chosen elsewhere. But where?

(5) Certain results of the investigation indicate a solution: 45 per cent of leaders were more or less linked to the capital (even the landowners chosen lived in San Juan) as against 20·2 per cent living in the village. Better still, 78·3 per cent were the sons of non-residents as against 5·4 per cent of leaders whose parents were born in Pocito. Let us leave aside the question whether new aspirations and desires for change are oriented toward a class egoism. These last statistics indicate that the individuals most apt to understand change are those who are least rooted in the community and thus, relative to it, the most marginal. If we proceed now from folk to Indian communities, we see that empirical research confirms our last conclusion even more clearly.

H. G. Barnett concludes from three experiences of acculturation —among the Yorok, Hupa and Karok—that a desire for novelties brought by the whites is manifested most clearly among individuals, especially half-breeds, whose behaviour shows them to be culturally maladjusted. Widows also seem, often because of their peripheral position, to form an avant-garde in accepting Euro-American culture. Prestige, in these circumstances, is not a determining factor of general acceptance of a new trait, since half-breeds—far from enjoying prestige—are rejected both by whites and by Indians, and occupy an eccentric, ill-viewed, and criticised position in the population.

But it is precisely because they are maladjusted and have personal conflicts they cannot resolve in terms of their own customs, that these people will tend to imitate 'foreigners' to see if their customs will allow them to find a resolution of their own dissatisfactions. What Barnett shows is that it is the 'unsatisfied, maladjusted, frustrated and incompetent' who are the 'first to accept cultural innovation and change'.[13]

It remains to be understood how these innovations spread from such people to the rest of the group, a phenomenon that is all the more strange since they are themselves rejected. For obviously, they can only be chosen as leaders if, having changed themselves, they can cause others to change. Barnett's studies of the Indians of California and the North-west Coast seem to suggest that to comprehend this phenomenon of generalisation, one must take into account not only the existence but the proportion of half-breeds. At the onset of contact, when there were still few half-breeds, these were finally absorbed by the indigenous culture. It is necessary for their number to increase, and for the indigenous group to feel that it is threatened, and that it is becoming heterogeneous, before instability passes from individuals to the collectivity, which then enters a crisis phase. It is then and only then that, as culturally marginal individuals, half-breeds can become innovative leaders.

We reach a similar conclusion in following the reasoning of Murphy[14] who, while giving a prominent role to marginal men in social change, explains that this change cannot spread from them to the community at large until that community is in a state of crisis. In a crisis situation, he who does not have a sense of personal conflict is unlikely to seek a solution; he is tossed about by events. It is the most maladjusted person then who has the strongest sense of the necessary transformations to put into operation, and the urgency of adherence to new values.

It is because the whole society is in crisis—and suffers more or less consciously from its anomie—that the honoured chiefs or experienced elders will fail to find a way to save the population from the growing general dissatisfaction, and those who formerly had the least prestige will take their revenge by becoming leaders for change. Which in turn means that we are dealing with the phenomenon of 'circulation of elites'. But it is always necessary to bypass prestige for progress to be generalised.

It is clearer now why cultural anthropology had to change the meaning given to marginality without, however, denying the pathological character attributed to marginal men. When that definition was being formulated, the marginal men were rejected by all. They had to wait until Indian society was in a period of crisis (that is, when the acculturative processes, having begun, had only reached the stage of disaggregation of former communities, but had not reached that of their reconstruction) for marginal individuals to have a useful role to play. They became, by virtue of their very marginality, the leaders of these new communities, which had ceased to have confidence in their chiefs and elders, since they were powerless before the situation of de-structuration that their groups had entered.

We must add to this—to the change of the sociological position of Indian villages—the sad failure of American anthropologists in their first attempts at modernisation. Sometimes the chiefs and elders rejected progress, feeling instinctively that it threatened their advantages and privileges, and that the *status quo* was thus preferable. At others—especially in the case of large landholders or feudal political chiefs—they accepted those new culture traits they were offered, but only for the benefit of their own stratum, and opposed their dissemination. They broadened the gap between those who were at the top of the hierarchy and those below. Progress, jealously guarded by a handful of men, can only lead to the proletarisation and the alienation of the mass. Anthropologists overcame their first failure by the discovery of a possible new elite, one which was followed all the more when the culture contact was expressed as anomie equally uncomfortable for all. But it should be noted that in this reversal of perspectives, it was marginal individuals and not marginal groups that were vindicated.

Should we not go further? It seems to me that there is a trend toward granting an important function and role to certain marginal societies in the politics of planned acculturation. Freyre, as early as twenty years ago, presented a defence of the *mocambos* (a certain sort of hovel) of the Pernambuco region of Brazil. Today we find anthropologists recognising the value of peripheral quarters, even of the 'bidonvilles' of some large South American cities, because they allow a better relationship between the migrant peasant family and the exigencies of urban life. Firstly, the price of cheap land, even the possibility of acquiring it, assures these migrants the ownership of their houses, without having to pay out money every month, and so gives them a sense of security that helps them to confront more successfully the traumas that would be generated by life in the metropolitan centre.[15]

Secondly, in re-establishing the village community, or creating one that closely resembles it, with its effective solidary relationships, mutual aid and festivals, these peripheral quarters provide a good transition. Here the new urban behavioural forms—which are taught to children at school and to adults in factories—can be internalised progressively, without serious problems for the personality undergoing acculturation. True, for impatient planners, these poorly-integrated areas remain shocking. But we begin to understand that they in fact constitute the least costly of initiations into new life-styles and the homogenisation of national cultures.

In conclusion, half-way between the vindication of marginal individuals and marginal groups, we can cite an interesting quotation from Bert Hoselitz:

> 'The important role of marginal individuals in the economic activities of underdeveloped countries is clearly shown today. We can cite the case of the Chinese in many countries in South Asia, and that of the Indians in West Africa, the Lebanese and Syrian merchants in West Africa, Latin America and other underdeveloped regions.'[16]

If we have left this observation to the end, it is because it belongs more to the sociology of development than to applied anthropology, and also because it, in fact, involves marginal individuals or groups less than it does ethnic minorities in plural societies. Such minorities can certainly further progress, but more often their only concern is their own profit—they remain culturally 'encysted'. So, though the text quoted appears at first to confirm the importance of marginality in culture change, in fact it is ultimately outside our thesis—the natives in all such cases receiving only the crumbs of the feast that is eaten by others, exactly as in the colonial epoch.

The development of the so-called 'marginal group'—which I prefer to call the 'minority group', which is not at all the same thing—occurs at the expense of, and delays that of the national community and the mass of the autochthonous occupants of the soil who find themselves further and further removed to the periphery of progress, so that in the end the term 'marginal' or 'marginalised' suits them more than it does the enterprising minorities that coexist with them.

NOTES

1. Redfield, Linton and Herskovits, *Memorandum*, op. cit.
2. R. Maunier, *Sociologie Coloniale*, Tome I, Domat Montchrestien, Paris, 1932.
3. See G. Freyre, *O Mundo que o Portugues creou*, J. Olympio, Rio de Janeiro, 1940; *Uma politica transnacional de cultura para o Brasil de hoje*, ed. da Rev. Bras. de Estudos Politicos, Minas Gerais, 1960; *Aventura e Rotina*, Livres de Brasil, Lisbon, no date.
4. G. Freyre, *Maîtres et Esclaves*, tr. fr. Gallimard, Paris, 7th ed., 1952.
5. Cf. D. W. Jeffreys, 'Some Rules of Directed Culture Change Under Catholicism', *Amer. Anthrop.*, 58, 4, 1956.
6. Juan A. Ortega y Medina, 'Ideas de la evangelización anglo-sajona entre los indigenas de los Astados Unidos de Norte America', *Amer. Indigena*, 18, 2, 1958.
7. The most typical example of this point of view is that of E. V. Stonequist, *The Marginal Man*, Charles Scribner's & Sons, New York, 1937.
8. R. Bastide, 'Le principe de coupure de la comportement afro-brésilien', *Anais de XXXI Congresso Intern. de Americanistas*, S. Paulo, Anhembi, 1955.
9. G. Balandier, personal communication.

10. H. Hyman, 'The Psychology of Status', *Arch. de Psych.*, 38, 1942.
11. E. Williams, *Assimilação e populações marginais do Brasil*, S. Paulo, 1940.
12. *Desarrollo comunitario y combio social*, Consejo federal de inversiones, Buenos-Aires, 1965.
13. H. G. Barnett, 'Personal Conflicts and Culture Change', op. cit.
14. G. Murphy, *Personality: A Biosocial Approach to Origins and Structure*, Harper & Bros., New York, 1947.
15. J. C. Turner, 'La marginalidad urbana: calamidad o solucion?', *Desarrollo Economico*, Mexico, 3-3.4, 1966.
16. B. Hoselitz, 'Les principaux concepts de l'analyse des répercussions sociales dans l'évolution technique', in *Industrialisation et Société*, UNESCO, 1963.

Applied Anthropology and Development Sociology

7

We have previously provided a conception of what applied anthropology is by discussing its ends, means and leaders. But this conception is still only an approximate one. Now it must be clarified, and the best way of doing this seems to be to compare it with something else which, though not identical to that conception, is like it, often confused with it, and even conflicts with it.

Firstly, we must distinguish it from development sociology. We have already seen that development sociology tends to dominate the anthropological perspective in Russia, but we must also add that, as we shall show, an analagous movement exists in the United States. The clearest symptom of this change of disciplinary interest—or of this confusion about the boundaries of these two domains—is the current tendency shown by Americans to replace the term 'acculturation' by that of 'social', 'economic' or 'cultural' change, in their work and their ethnological publications.

In applied anthropology, at least until very recently, emphasis was placed on the exogenous nature of sources of modernisation and, consequently, on the significance of culture contact. The problem then became one of eliminating obstacles that sprang from too violent oppositions between different civilisations. This recalls the dialogue between a European who had just landed on the shores of Brazil and a Tupenamba who was amazed by his energetic activities: 'Why go to such pains,' said the Tupenamba, 'when the earth provides everything a man needs to live?' 'I am not amassing wealth for myself but for my children,' replied the European. 'Well then, your children are ill-bred if you work so hard for them when they should be working for you and caring for you in your old age.'

105

Or again, there is the following song of a modern-day Australian, recorded by Fisk:[1]

SONG OF THE TRIBAL ECONOMIST

The primitive farmer says cash
Is unsatisfactory trash;
    It won't keep off rain
    And gives me a pain
If I use it to flavour my hash.

So why should I work out my guts
At the whim of these government mutts,
    My liquor comes free
    From the coconut tree
And my Mary makes cups from the nuts.

Should I walk for three days into town,
Sell a sack of my spuds for a crown,
    Buy a bottle of beer
    And fall flat on my ear?
No, I'd rather stay here and lie down.

If I act in a rational way
I'll just sit on my backside today.
    When I want a good feed
    I've got all I need
Piping hot, and there's nothing to pay.

Cash cropping is all very well
If you've *got* to have something to sell;
    But tell me, sir, why
    If there's nothing to buy
Should I bother? You can all go to hell.

Development sociology studies the transition of a backward, traditional or feudal society into a modern and industrialised one with commercialised agriculture and a so-called 'democratic' political regime. The problem involved is to eliminate such obstacles as retard historical evolution, or slow down economic growth.

Applied anthropology tends to emphasise the importance of cultural factors and of mentalities which must be changed so that social structures may change. Thus, Catholic missionaries working in an Andean community thought it would be advisable first to treat bodies, and later, souls. Without seeking to convert, they brought a whole series of technical devices borrowed from white civilisation, to relieve the hard physical labour of the inhabitants. But these new traits—which would have improved agricultural productivity, given women more leisure, and resulted in a more balanced diet—were not accepted. So these missionaries then realised that proselytism must precede economic change. They would have to give the natives, by fostering a new mentality, a sense of the dignity of the human individual in a society where only the collectivity and not the individual had value.

Development sociology, on the contrary, accents economic change which should bring about social-structural changes and, through them, changes in mentality. The order of these two approaches is precisely inverse. The indigenous supersedes the exogenous. So its effects on this sociology will be:

(1) To define the criteria of underdevelopment, which may be of the economic order (e.g. per capita income of inhabitants, subsistence agriculture), of the demographic order (high birth rate plus high infant mortality rate, plus a high mortality rate at all ages), or the social order (e.g. the sexual division of labour).

(2) To define internal and structural obstacles to economic development, e.g., the egalitarian aspects of the productive sector, with the law of sumptuary consumption imposed on those who set themselves apart from the mass; the kinship system as a basis of role allocation, which prevents role-correspondence, since a modern economy cannot emerge until lineages or extended families are replaced by nuclear families and the latter compete for higher status; in brief, with the transition to contractural rights from rights determined at birth, and by birth order.[2]

(3) To define the criterion of social development, that is, of the effects of economic change on structures. The criteria most frequently chosen are increased diversification, professional specialisation, and role-differentiation. While in a traditional society, roles ascribed to individuals are few and the familial, religious, economic and political ones are merged, in a developed society, these diverse forms of activity are separated, the norms governing them are specific and no longer diffuse. The increase of productivity in effect demands a more extensive division of labour and this first specialisation is finally reflected in other sectors of the society. From the economy, a redistribution of functions spreads, and these, formerly fused, become separate.

Another criterion put forward—and which defines democracy in contradistinction to folk societies or patrimonial regimes—is vertical mobility of individuals, who can as likely descend, because of laziness, traditionalism, etc., as rise along the social ladder through their efforts or initiative and especially through education.

These two movements—toward differentiation and mobility— when joined, cause the social stratification system to change in its turn. While in traditional societies there may exist only one upper and directing class, in modern societies there is diversification of elites—union, political, economic, cultural, military. They are recruited among different classes which are being formed, and thus often have conflicting interests. In any case, they are formed on the basis of individual competence, and no longer of birth.[3]

(4) The methodology of applied anthropology will be more qualitative than quantitative, since it studies the impact of one culture on another, these cultures being considered as *gestalts*. Better yet, it would affirm, with Malinowski in his study of the Christian Bantu family in South Africa, that the new family that emerges from these contacts is neither the traditional Bantu family, nor the Christian European family, nor a combination of the two; but a completely original entity, *sui generis*, and that as a result, it must be described in its essential newness if it is to be understood.

The methodology of development sociology will, on the contrary, be quantitative, clearly so at the level of economic expansion, which can be measured, but also at the level of social change, through sampling—which should be as representative as possible—of different groups according to their socio-economic level, the occupations of their members, their residential patterns, their status, and their function in the global society. This then allows analysis of the degree of differentiation obtained, the degree of vertical mobility, and of elite formation. Also, it will employ opinion poles on this same basis, so as to elucidate the special needs of each of these groups, their aspirations, their perspectives on the future, and their capacity for action within the global society.[4]

The mathematical nature of development sociology—as opposed to the more qualitative nature of applied anthropology—shows up most clearly in studies of the economic aspect of development. Failures of growth models constructed in our Western societies when applied to underdeveloped countries have not discouraged planners. In effect, they conclude that their models were merely too simple, and that other variables were at play in the Third World, but that to use a computer to handle more data on real phenomena sufficed to come to grips with the total reality. But the necessity for speed forced them to use incomplete models. And especially here, the hazards of political decision-making were translated into further failures.

In the first instance, they failed because planners always started with existing models that had worked in analagous cases, content merely to introduce modifications when they should have created completely new models. In the second instance, they failed because the manipulation of computerised data by men with political power was unforeseeable. From this situation grew a new technique in development sociology: experts now do 'simulated' studies by means of computers and programmes to reveal possible outcomes, from which the politicians may then choose.

We need not emphasise the limitations of these methods, for the will of some men can do nothing against mass resistance. And only the ethnologist can analyse the latter, to find responses to it. All we wish to show is that development sociology, even or especially as it improves, is still essentially quantitative, and thus becomes increasingly far removed from applied anthropology.

(5) It is on the basis of opinion polls—or economic statistics on prices, salaries, productivity, imports and exports, national or individual income—that development strategies can be elaborated. But such strategies must be implemented by the state. While, as we have seen, applied anthropology has taken a microscopic point of view, development sociology has a national and therefore a macroscopic one. This in turn means that it is essentially centralist; it is the government that elaborates and implements its plans. True, governments of underdeveloped countries may call on foreign experts— both economists and anthropologists—but these anthropologists will only be asked to judge the internal obstacles to the plan's application.

Another factor encourages centralisation, namely the existence of destructive, as well as constructive, effects of development. If the economic forces released by it are allowed free play, and are not controlled, their disorganisational effects may become extreme: exodus from the countryside to towns, leading to unemployment, juvenile delinquency, and prostitution; vertical mobility resulting in more descents than rises; a growing gap between the privileged minority and a mass which will have to become 'proletarianised' . . . How is it possible to ensure transition from one structure to another without serious disorganisation, if not through the control of men in power over the societal change they have instituted, and for which they are responsible?

(6) This control should also be continuous, as is shown at the other pole of the continuum that goes from the capitalist type of development—the only one we have discussed so far—to the socialist type of development. For if the revolution has allowed a raising of the status of the working or peasant class, it has not prevented the formation within that class of an elite group of workers or peasants, more qualified by education and by its selection system—and then for members of this stratum with higher status, to aid their children or relatives to obtain better opportunities—and leading finally to the formation of a bureaucratic class. From the formal point of view then, there is little difference between the ends envisaged and the content of these sorts of plans.

Industrialisation always proceeds in the direction of differentiation and vertical mobility of individuals and groups, and it necessitates not only development planning but the control of this by the central government or a single party, in all the countries where it is introduced.

But over and above these formal analogies, there is an opposition within the epistemological perspective—the same in the case of development sociology as we found in that of planned acculturation—dialectic *versus* functionalism. (And this is aside from the opposed ends, namely the implantation of a capitalist system or of state industry.)

The point of departure of the American sociologists is that every social system is structured to meet certain exigencies so as to preserve its stability. The exigencies it must meet are: the production of sufficient resources for the life of its members; maintenance of interactional norms; control of collective behaviour that could affect society; preservation and transmission of a certain number of values from generation to generation. This means that planning consists in making a society pass from a preindustrial to an industrial system without affecting basic exigencies, merely by providing different institutions which will meet them equally well.[5]

The point of departure of Soviet sociologists is that social structures in the final analysis depend on the forces and relations of production; that the real state of these forces and relations in a preindustrial society is produced by its history; and that consequently, it is through study of these historical sequences that the transformation of such a society into an industrial one can be planned in a truly scientific manner.

(7) However, development sociology is undergoing a significant mutation, at least development sociology established in Western and especially, American, milieux. For despite all the plans and programmes maturely elaborated by specialists, the gap between the underdeveloped (or even developing) and the developed countries, far from narrowing, has widened. And thus, this sort of sociology must have neglected a fundamental variable that explains development. Naturally, it is the sociologists of the under-

developed countries—Africa and particularly Latin America—who will be called upon to bring to light the behaviour and significance of this variable.

A country may become industrialised without that industrialisation bringing with it the anticipated profits. From this comes the idea that underdevelopment is not due only to obstacles from the traditional society, but that development is conditioned by international relations. It cannot be detached from other industrial societies (the US, Russia, or the richer European nations) which only develop a backward country in order to profit from it by relying on certain national sectors of these underdeveloped countries.

This, in turn, means that development sociology is transforming itself into the 'sociology of dependence'. But to be formed, this new sociology needs to break with the general concepts of traditional social science, since these concepts in the end allow only a simple justification of dependence, having been forged by sociologists from the developed countries. Thus, the sociology of change should in the end bring about the preliminary change of sociology.[6] This has not yet begun, so we shall stop here.

We have said enough for the reader to be able to see that development sociology and applied anthropology are not to be confused; the former has its own field, and different methodology and concerns. But if these two disciplines are distinct, that does not mean that they cannot cooperate. This is all the more true since, as we saw in the historical chapter, applied anthropology since the Second World War has had to take on international responsibilities, e.g., industrial conflict and mass media propaganda. Consequently, cultural anthropology has enlarged its field from the study of small-scale communities to so-called complex societies like our own.

Development sociology does, at a certain point, consider the problem of culture contact, or at least that of what are usually termed sub-cultures. An example is that of the confrontation between urban and rural cultures in the same nation. Previously, relations between town and country were discussed in terms of opposition, but today they are described in terms of continuity;

the countryside can only realise its potential by making use of the town. But the urbanisation of rural areas involves their acculturation,[7] and so applied anthropology must be called in. The confrontation and the class struggle between workers and bourgeois does not preclude that—especially in our consumer societies—this struggle should take place through a whole series of communications and exchanges which may at first seem antithetical.

The old populist culture dies, but is not replaced by a proletarian one, but rather it is contaminated by that of the proximate petite bourgeoisie. Gablot, in his book on the barrier and the level, (*La Barrière et le Niveau*) characterises this progressive levelling effect of the proletariat upon the petite bourgeoisie as the effort of the latter to establish barriers at another level. At any rate, what matters here is that the class struggle takes place at the same time as the progressive assimilation of non-proletarian values—resulting in a cultural change of the working mass—and consequently this situation poses a relevant question for applied anthropology rather than development sociology.

It is not coincidental that at the beginning of her book, *The Second Sex*, Simone de Beauvoir compares the position of women with that of Jews and Negroes—that is to those positions that are generally of more interest to anthropology than to sociology. And it seems, in reading that book, that the liberation of women in a society created by and for men does not occur through the creation of a feminist culture—at once opposed to and complementing masculine culture—but through the assimilation of women into that masculine culture considered to be privileged.

We could make similar observations about youth. Scarcely twenty years ago, 'youth' meant only a normal process in the development of learning, a prolonged period, consequently, during which young people were stabilised in that ambiguous state of adolescence and 'dependence,' whereas their elders, at the same age, had already held positions of responsibility. Recently, an attempt has been made to create a sub-culture of youth, that could be called the 'Yé-Yé' culture.* To a certain extent, the rebellion

* Roughly equivalent to the 'rock culture'.

of youth—like those of women, workers, rural people—has been not only sociological but cultural, the expression of an acculturative desire on their part, and in this case, for assimilation to the culture of adults.

In sum, the social upheavals we see now, within the so-called 'developed' world, are of the same kind as those occurring in the Third World. They are the reflection not only of social structural changes, but also of the effects of encounters—within the great nations—between heterogeneous sub-cultures, revealing the same processes that one finds in the relations between city and country, workers and bourgeois, males and females, or young and old. These processes of resistance, syncretism, reinterpretation, assimilation, and of counter-acculturation are what we have already found in the relationships between heterogeneous ethnic cultures.

Several examples should suffice to illustrate this consistence of phenomena, which remains for us the most important lesson of anthropology—which we have emphasised in comparing planned acculturation in the capitalist and socialist contexts. Despite the opposition of ends and development strategies in each of these types of case, the same laws are still at work, and the same regularities revealed. This is also true for the sorts of cases we have just cited: the phenomenon of 'reinterpretation' whereby the petit bourgeois reinterpret the portraits in the ancestral galleries of the old nobility via the family photo album (and in the same conventional poses); the phenomenon of 'resistance', whereby the pseudo-proletariat shapes itself according to the image others have of it, which proudly lays claim both to everything that distinguishes it and for which it is reproached, above all, that which distinguishes it from an 'embourgeoised' proletariat; the phenomenon of 'syncretism', whereby this proletariat copies the fashions of the petite bourgeoisie while maintaining, nevertheless, a certain number of the values of the old populist class.

Or again, there is the new class of cultivators who, while having changed their outlook and acquired a sense of commercial profit, still remain in many ways a continuum of the old peasant class, from which they have inherited and retained certain kinds of behaviour. Finally, there is the phenomenon of 'counter-acculturation', which can go so far as to take messianic forms (Hippies) or apocalyptic ones, as in certain revolutionary youth movements.

These consistencies permit us to conclude that applied anthropology has a wider field than that to which it has sometimes been relegated, namely that of planning decolonisation. (And it is curious to note the extension of the term 'colonialism' to all the situations we have just enumerated, or nearly all: colonisation of the country by the towns, of women by men. And has not a Minister of Education even spoken of 'decolonising' the university?)

On the contrary, applied anthropology can make a most important contribution to all the phenomena that follow on, or are the effects of development, and which development sociology chooses to ignore. It seems to us that criminology already gained something when it discovered—or rediscovered—that there is a criminal sub-culture, with its own norms of conduct, system of sanctions (positive and negative), its own structures of interpersonal relations. Development sociology would certainly have something to gain there also.

In our opinion, the main problem of this development sociology—the tragic actuality of which has been recalled to us by certain recent events—is that of knowing whether there is one pattern of development or whether it is not necessary to multiply the patterns in accordance with ethnic lines. True, one cannot deny that with the reduction of distance, the increasing speed of communication, the growing identity of economic models, the pressure of the mass media, the world is tending to form a closed cultural system.

Lalande maintained against Spencer, more than half a century ago, that involution or homogenisation was replacing evolution. However, Lefebvre rightly asks whether ethnic cultures are definitely condemned to 'folklorisation'—whether the historical reality of a culture will let itself so readily be reduced to nothing, or whether, following an incontestable period of crisis (which to me is marked by the success of development sociology versus applied anthropology) cultural diversification, based on diversities of historical evolution and the multiplicity of languages, will not reappear. 'It is indeed possible,' he writes in a passage in which the prophet displaces the Marxist, 'that what began as a period of homogenisation, characterised by the predominance of techniques, structures and homologous systems, is now ending.'[8]

It is equally true that this pluralisation of roads toward development, this 'culturisation' of phases of economic growth poses problems, for the risks remain of sinking into false analogies, such as that between the communal type of mutual aid and a cooperative system (which latter supposes the existence among the co-operators of a capitalist mentality, turned toward the more or less long-term future) or that between the absence of individual ownership of the means of production—or finally that of so-called 'primitive democracy' with democracies of the representative type.

An economist concerned about creating an economic typology of societies writes: 'development strategies conceived by the countries of the Third World see, by definition, a transformation of structures. But this transformation should proceed by the adaptation rather than by the destruction of existing institutions.' But he also adds that in this desire to utilise certain existing cultural traits for a politics of development, simplified schemas have been formulated 'under the pretext of burning bridges', which identify the absence of antagonistic social classes of owners and non-owners with the absence of inequality within the group.

> 'All modalities of collective labour have been praised, including those which in reality constitute veritable corvées. All forms of cooperation have been encouraged, including those which lead to the freezing of relationships of inequality characteristic of the extended family dominated by the gerontocracy, and of villages with a structure of clearly-differentiated classes, led by an elite that monopolises all positions of influence in the local hierarchy, and especially the eventual administration of the cooperative.'[9]

These phenomena of petrification recall a statement by Berque whom we have cited above, and who, extolling the return to 'sources', to the spontaneous forces of living cultures, as they struggle against the constraining or deteriorating aspects of development, still distinguishes between the 'original' (that which is 'authentic, original or if you will, immortal, as the gesture man makes in directing the flow of the spring, or planting a tree; that cannot be nor should it be disavowed')—and the traditional ('while tradition should be repudiated not because it preserves the old, but because it corrupts and exploits it—to maintain man's forward movement, it seems necessary to break with his continuity'). And he extols as a result 'an energetic looking back' but one which is not for all that 'a naïve return to origins'.[10]

In a word, these two authors whom we have just cited wish— as against the rigidity of a single system of development, instituted by Western sociology and economics—to leave the door open to a pluralism of development. But this pluralism can only be conceived as a double process; the adaptation of development to the diverse cultures and civilisations of man and the distinction within them of that which is living, dynamic, and authentic from that which is only petrified, weighty and ultimately alienating tradition. This adaptation and distinction can only be the work of the applied anthropologist, and not of the sociologist alone—even less of the economist. Or else, development sociology must expand and in the end, in order to succeed, demand recourse to applied anthropology.

It was the Asian thinkers, like Ghandi, and closer to us the theoreticians of negritude in Francophonic countries and of African personality in Anglophonic countries[11] who first argued against the Marxists on the two following points:

(a) Culture is not an epiphenomenon. It is the constructive work of man, just as is technology, in which it does not burn itself out.

(b) A return to sources is necessary. Asia and Africa need not copy the white world, but should discover, in returning to their origins, their own developmental models. Doubtless, the young newly-independent nations can only survive on condition that they adopt other methods of production and distribution of wealth.

But they must adapt these to Asiatic or African traditions which will give to all these novelties a different meaning than the one they have for us. It is clear that this desire for culturisation and the search for an original road to progress for Asians and Africans, with their famous 'African Socialism'[12] for example, still remains ambiguous in not having distinguished as does Berque the 'original' from the 'traditional'.

At bottom, two conceptions of culture are at play here. The first would reify (in the Marxian sense of the term) a particular archaic tradition, that which is based on collective labour, the absence of personal property, lineage organisation, and which defines as 'socialist' the spirit of that tradition. This means that the duty of the politicians, in their struggle against the prolonging of colonisation, is a turning backward, toward a world seen as paradise for which the Asian or African retains an incurable nostalgia.[13]

Kwame Nkrumah rightly says of this first conception of culture that it makes a fetish out of the communal type of African society.[14] But there is another conception of culture, which sees it as a 'productive soul' and not as a collection of culture traits, nor yet as an 'expression' of a particular philosophy of life, and not as a congealed tradition. It is obviously reasonable that technology should not be substituted for cultures. For a soulless technology, as Bergson emphasised, is the worst sort of alienation. It must become humanised by incarnating itself into the rich diversity of ethnic cultures. But these cultures are seen now as incessant upsurgings of life, productive of and nourishing the new, as the authentic originality, and no longer reduced to the organisational forms that they produced at a given point in time, and which tradition—perhaps even that colonisation against which they must struggle—has hardened or fossilised. Culture is seen, in a word, as fire and spirit, not as a skeleton or hardened lava.

It is clear that, in a parallel perspective, applied anthropology regains all its rights. And does not everything we have just noted as applying to Asia and Africa apply to Europe, even within the various Soviet and socialist republics, when certain of them proclaim their right to discover the national path that will lead them to Communism, when they too affirm the cultural pluralism of development?

Basically, certain observers may consider the Czechoslovakian revolt as 'the expression of the inadaptability of one social model directly and mechanically transported from the Soviet experience of the thirties', of an ethnicity that had another history, and its own world of values. It was seen by the young Czeck opposition itself, as a return to the young Marx, who refused to define human productivity as creating only new means and relations of production, but also as creating culture. The transplanting of the Soviet model amongst them was certainly recognised as that of an economic and social system devoted to a greater efficiency of production and a greater justice in the apportioning of wealth; but one which neglected the major truth that the liberation of the dominated and exploited man should serve only toward a greater expansion of his creative liberty, that is, of his cultural possibilities.

This new insistence on going from simple material, economic and social development to the cultural—at once based on the history of an ethnicity and conceived as a source of the new—while already comprised in development sociology as we have defined it, here again borders on anthropology.

NOTES

1. E. K. Fisk, 'Planning in a Primitive Economy: From Pure Subsistence to the Production of a Market Surplus', *The Economic Record*, June, 1964.
2. N. S. Eisenstadt, 'Changes in Patterns of Stratification Attendant on Attainment of Political Independence', *Transactions of the Third World Congress of Sociology*, Vol. III, London, Int. Sociol. Assoc., 1956.
3. B. F. Hoselitz, 'La estratificacion social y el desarrollo economico', and S. M. Lipset, 'Problemo de la investigacion y analisis comparado de la movilidad y el desarrollo', *America*

Latina, Rio de Janeiro, VII, I, 1964. Talcott Parsons, 'Some Considerations in the Theory of Social Change', *Rural Sociology*, XXVI, 3, 1961.

4. Programmes of the International Studies Center of the Massachusetts Institute of Technology.

5. B. F. Hoselitz, op. cit.

6. Cf. Theotonio dos Santos, 'Sous-développpment et sciences sociales', *Hermes*, 3, 1966; Costa Pinto, 'La sociologie du changement et le changement de la sociologie', *Eudena*, Buenos-Aires, 1963; A. Gunder Frank, 'Sociology of Development and Underdevelopment of Sociology', *Catalyst*, Univ. of Buffalo, 3, Summer, 1967; F. Henrique Cardoso, 'Analyses sociologiques du développpment économique', *Rev. Latino-americaine de Sociol.*, Buenos-Aires, 1, 2, 1965.

7. P. Rambaud, *Société rurale et urbanisation*, Éditions du Seuil, Paris, 1969.

8. H. Lefebvre, *Critique de la Vie quotidienne*, 2nd ed., D'Arche, Paris, 1958, and especially, *Posidon: contre les technocrates—en finir avec l'humanité-fiction*, Gonthier, Geneva, 1967.

9. Ignacy Sachs, *La Découverte du Tiers Monde,* Flammarion, Paris, 1971.

10. J. Berque, op. cit.

11. It is curious to note that the theory of african personality is much more exclusive and rigid than that of negritude which, above all, with Senghor, calls for a merging of cultures and human research as opposed to ethnic research.

12. See L. V. Thomas, *Le socialisme et l'Afrique*, 2 vols., Paris, 1966, and especially the pages devoted to Senghor.

13. Julius Nyrere, *Freedom and Unity*, Oxford University Press, Oxford, 1966, and *Ujamaa, the Basis of African Socialism*, Dar-es-Salaam, 1962 (mimeo.)

14. Kwame N'Krumah, 'African Socialism Revisited', *African Forum*, I, 3, New York, 1966.

Applied Anthropology and Applied Ethnology

If the distinction between applied anthropology and development sociology was relatively simple to establish, the same is not true for its difference from applied ethnology; we feel that none of our preceding chapters has made the latter emerge clearly enough. This is no doubt because the anthropologists who were called upon to act in this connection were also ethnographers, working in communities which were strictly delimited geographically and culturally. The distinction is nonetheless of major importance, and we must devote several pages to it.

The idea that dominates applied ethnography is that the population which is undergoing change (and exogenous change at that) is more important than the development-scheme which is being introduced into its community. Firstly, because the scheme, no matter what it is, will only be accepted if it meets real needs experienced by the local population. Otherwise, no matter how 'elegant' it may be, it will fail. Secondly, because even if it is attractive to the population, even in agreeing about the ends to be pursued, they cannot be in agreement with the means for their realisation, since the means—though indissolubly linked to the ends in the planner's terms—disrupt the former habits to which the people are attached.

It is therefore necessary, not only before implementing a scheme, but before creating it, to begin with a careful study of the population on which one wishes to act, to know its culture in all its details and in all sectors, which is precisely the task of the ethnographer. Only he, after a patient and painstaking investigation, will be able to say what needs are felt, what collective representations there are, and to describe the possible communication network for transmitting information (which changes from one social structure to another); to describe the value system or norms of conduct which may present resistance, and the limits of elasticity of that resistance (the system and limits of which also change from one culture, ethnicity, or villager to another).

We maintain that this should be an investigation of the population's social or cultural specifics which is both patient and painstaking. Students led by Sol Tax to an Indian village were so overwhelmed by the state of poverty in which the Indians were living that they wanted to act immediately, to proceed to apply a change-scheme promptly, without wasting time in a preliminary description of the culture of the village. Ethnographic investigation seemed a purely gratuitous activity to them, one which could and should be dispensed with since it merely put off the moment of liberation which was their ultimate goal.

Tax reports that he had great difficulty in getting them to admit that it was necessary first to describe objectively, and without emotion, the facts as they were, and that a preliminary knowledge of the milieu was necessary in order to be able to act effectively upon it. He thinks that his students probably thought him heartless, and that they remained basically convinced that a general and superficial acquaintance with the community would have been sufficient for a development programme even though, in a similar case where there was an imperfect knowledge of social organisation, and of the value and normative systems, the programme risked causing more harm than good to these Indians whom they wished to liberate from poverty.

The schema of community development strategy has been elaborated, starting from the idea that there is no development system which is universally valid, and that it is therefore necessary always to act empirically.[1] Here are its principal stages, in outline:

(1) First study the culture and the society of the population in such a way as to foresee whether that population is capable of changing and can do so without danger; in particular, if the development plan which is suggested is primarily economic and

technical in nature, it is necessary to compare the present technical and economic aspects of the culture with the conception of them as planned, through an in-depth study of the social and cultural milieu, to diagnose the foreseeable reactions to it, and to consider possible responses to them.

(2) To discover within the culture to be considered, the factors which could permit the facilitation of development; in particular, those which would permit the ones with vested interests to understand first the usefulness of change, then to arouse their enthusiasm for it. In sum, to get them to participate in the work of the experts or social engineers. In order to succeed, the ethnographer must, as we have said, mould the acculturative process to the very dynamic of the society, rather than impose it through force, from without.

(3) To follow the evolution of the community from day to day. For example, at the end of each day, in evening meetings, all the members of the team would share their experiences or discoveries, so as to inspect the mechanisms by which the development or acculturation takes place while it is actually in operation, without waiting until the possible resistant reactions have time to harden or to become institutionalised. It is necessary to detect them and propose solutions for each obstacle encountered on the way.

(4) Finally, after a certain length of time—varying according to the area and scheme—it is necessary to evaluate the results obtained in terms of the original programme.[2] This evaluation is absolutely indispensable, for if the results are not good, work must be started again, on other bases, after the reasons for setbacks or slowdowns have been found, instead of continuing the former strategy which was first followed by the team.

It is obvious that the task is a long one. Can it not be abbreviated? The only method which may be proposed to this end would be to choose, in each region, a representative community which would allow the applied ethnographer to extrapolate the results obtained to cover all similar communities. We know that, essentially, in the same region (whose cultural limits remain to be traced) if there are differences from one village to another, these are generally only in terms of low-level details (e.g., of dress, pronunciation of words, etc.), while social structures remain analogous and the values internalised by individuals are homogenous.

This holds true whether these villages belong to one ethnicity, thus rooted in one global culture (if their relative isolation has not lasted long enough to differentiate them profoundly from one another) or whether, by diffusion from one another, the same culture traits have been spread in one migration of peoples. And finally, it holds true whether the ecological milieu (dense forest, savannah, or steppe, mountain or plateau, dry or humid climate, hot or glacial) has imposed the same life-style on all, necessitating the adaptation—technical, economic and consequently social—of men to their environment.

The stages of applied ethnography to be distinguished become slightly more complicated, but they remain basically the same. Only the first and the last are bifurcated:

(1A) The ethnographer must traverse the region, outline its cultural frontiers, situate its transitional zones. In the region thus delimited, using both his own observation and statements from informants, he must discover a community considered to be the most representative of the group. If the region is heterogeneous, e.g., with agricultural and mining zones, highland and plains villages, he must choose a representative population within each of these subsections.

(1B) It is here that these representative communities must then be studied minutely. From then on, the stages which we have enumerated above—those of discovery of facilitating factors, of daily control of the play of acculturation and development, of evaluation after a certain lapse of time, of the results obtained— do not change. But to (4) is added:

(4A) If the results are considered to be good, one may extrapolate the strategy which has been followed in the model village to the group of all the villages of the region or sub-region.

Even though Tax has applied this ethnographic method as we have seen above, he himself has radically distinguished it from applied anthropology, so as to emphasise the advantages of the latter over the former.[3] He holds, in effect, that the more general a proposition, the greater is its validity, not only theoretically (which goes without saying) but also as applied to a particular situation. For example, knowledge of a particular tribe of Indians is less important than a knowledge of North American Indians generally, and the latter, in turn, is less important than that of the most general laws of human nature, society, culture, and the way in which culture is transmitted from generation to generation, or from population to population. The most necessary prerequisite then is not to have a good empirical description of the community one will try to influence, but to have a good general anthropological theory.

Tracing an evolutionary curve paralleling the progress of science and of applied anthropology, Tax reminds us that the scholar only observes facts in terms of a theory (specifically in terms of theoretical hypotheses inherited from his predecessors). He first interprets the data which he gathers concerning a particular situation—let us say social or cultural facts, so as to stay close to our own subject—in the light of these theories or these hypotheses. But these data, in order to take their place in a conceptual framework, force him to improve the latter in relation to his own experiences, to modify or deepen it. In the same way, social problems which require for their solution the intervention of the applied anthropologists, are recognised first as problems in general terms of interests, ends or values. The problems peculiar to a given situation cannot then be understood except in the light of these general interests, of these ends, and of these social values which will later be used by the administration, either in the selection of problems, or in the way they are to be resolved.

Finally, these two paths—that of the theory of cultural and social facts and that of the resolution of social problems, or acculturation—are joined. For a knowledge of social values allows the administrator to discover where the real problems lie; these problems will in turn require for their resolution the utilisation of theoretical knowledge elaborated by pure anthropology such that it constitutes a dialectical movement between concepts and facts:

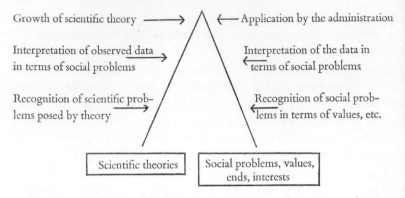

Growth of scientific theory ⟶ / ⟵ Application by the administration

Interpretation of observed data in terms of social problems ⟶ / ⟵ Interpretation of the data in terms of social problems

Recognition of scientific problems posed by theory ⟶ / ⟵ Recognition of social problems in terms of values, etc.

| Scientific theories | Social problems, values, ends, interests |

For his part, Clyde Kluckhohn comes to analogous conclusions when he gives the reasons for which the anthropologist is, from his point of view, superior to the sociologist or the economist in the realm of development and planning, even though he too makes mistakes. To follow his reasoning:

(1) The anthropologist is the only one who studies all the aspects of reality, from the biological and linguistic to techniques of work and social organisation. Furthermore, he studies them analytically, not as an ensemble of traits, but as constituting together organic configurations or systems in which everything is bound together. He is thus able to aid the specialist to understand the relation of his own specialty (e.g., economic life) to the total life of the community. But it is already obvious that he can only play this role because he has a theoretical conception of culture, and that it is this general conception which is applied in particular instances. 'To see the parts in relation to the whole is more important than to know all the details.'

(2) The anthropologist, in concentrating on cultural facts, shows that social institutions cannot exist apart from the individuals who participate in them, and that this participation in turn cannot exist without reference to value systems which belong to the social groups of which the individuals are members. He is thus able to help the specialist in social organisation, that is, the sociologist (and here we naturally mean the sociologist adept in the applied sociology of development) better to understand the resistance which

planned change may encounter and thus the necessity to take note in his calculations of the reactions of ethnic cultures. But it is obvious here as well that he can only fulfil this function in so far as he has a general theory of the relation between cultural and social facts, and because he has this general theory that he can apply it to particular, concrete situations.

(3) Thus—and this is Kluckhohn's own conclusion—applied anthropology cannot be confused with applied ethnography which is purely empirical; it consists in the application of the general concepts of pure anthropology to chosen situations.

Kluckhohn gives us a significant illustration of this point. The contribution of anthropology to the study of rural problems in the United States is not based on a greater initial familiarity with a given agricultural region, but rather on its investigation of structural and cultural models and on the knowledge of laws or mechanisms by which these models operate as total systems.

These conclusions—Tax's and Kluckhohn's—are thus aligned: knowledge of that which is to be changed is less important than general theoretical knowledge. It is this theoretical knowledge that the schools must provide to administrators or to development experts. It is now clearer, no doubt, why we have emphasised in this book the search for regularities, and the conceptual systematisation of the facts of acculturation. But we must add that, unfortunately, we still know very little of the laws of change.

At any rate, the failures of anthropologists derive less, it seems, from a lack of in-depth knowledge of one society or another (besides, it is impossible for an ethnographer to have complete understanding of the totality of a culture, even that of a small village with a small population; he must choose what seems most important and it is sufficient to compare various monographs on the same community to see the extent to which each one gives a different picture, one not always coherent with those given by others) than from the fact that anthropologists are still too poorly armed from the point of view of theory to be able to give applied anthropology a solid base on which to rest.

It is clear that to administrators or governments who call upon planning experts, the affirmation that general theoretical knowledge is more important, for the experts themselves, than an intimate knowledge of one or another ethnic group in its origins and specificity, will seem like a lack of common sense. And to a certain extent they will be right. We in no way wish to deny the value of applied ethnography, but to place it—both hierarchically and chronologically—in relation to applied anthropology. Hierarchically, ethnography can only come second, and as a subsidiary subject; for it is not sufficient to know a specific society well to know how to change it at the lowest cost. Its change, in effect, cannot occur without following certain theoretical laws, in terms of a preliminary understanding of what a culture is, the mechanisms of its functioning, its transmission and its dynamic of evolution. Without this theoretical knowledge, there would be a gap between empirical knowledge on the one hand, and the plan to be implemented on the other, which nothing could bridge—neither the empirical data which the ethnographer has enumerated, but which naturally have no directionality, nor the plan itself, which remains apart from and above them.

Further, chronologically, it is evident that applied ethnography cannot be an applied monography (a monograph is a set of statements of fact, not an orientation), but it may be an application of applied anthropology—applied to a specific ethnographic situation. The study of that ethnographic situation can therefore only come after, and not before.

In any case, in this work we keep to the idea of a general applied anthropology. What meaning must we give it? Before proposing our definition, other considerations must detain us for a moment; other paths, already followed in certain directions, must have our attention and our criticism.

NOTES

1. Cf. for example, Kavadias.
2. On the methods and the rules of substantive evaluation in the

social sciences and particularly the development sciences, see *Bulletin International des Sciences Sociales*, UNESCO, Vol. VII, 3, 1955.

3. Sol Tax, 'Anthropology and Administration', op. cit.

4. C. Kluckhohn, *Mirror for Man*, op. cit.

It might seem surprising that a chapter of this book should be devoted to envisaging the relationship between applied anthropology and structuralism. Yet, does not applied anthropology have as its aim the changing of the structures of society so as to cause it to evolve toward other patterns of relations between men and between groups? Is it not dialectical and diachronic, while structuralism, on the other hand, is synchronic? It is precisely because applied anthropology seeks to 'change' structures that it must first know them, weigh the resistant forces which they manifest, and study their formative laws since the aim of the policymaker is not to change what is for the pleasure of change, but rather with the view of substituting for a former social equilibrium —condemned in the name of certain values—a new one, thought to be better.

Today there is doubtless a tendency to credit man with a thaumaturgic power which makes him like a creator-god or a maker of worlds. Nowhere has this tendency appeared so strong as in Africa, exactly because the new states which have created themselves there do not represent an already-extant reality—either a nation, an historic tradition or a homogeneous culture—but more a future-oriented 'will' to found a patriotism, assert a national history, and unify tribal cultures. 'First seek political rule', proclaims Nkrumah, 'and the rest will be given you in abundance.' Political rule, that is to say, control over ends. . . .[1] For the politician cannot create new structures from nothing or, more exactly, only from the concepts of his reason or the images of his constructive imagination. He must take facts into account.

Here we may quote the famous example of the Asiatic mode of

production taken *stricto sensu,* and based essentially on large hydraulic works, state control of production and economic exchange, and a general tendency toward theocracy. We do not wish to enter into a discussion of this mode of production, or to join the debate that has engaged Godelier and Dhoquois in France. We wish simply to emphasise that—despite the 'tempests of the political region' which shook this regime from time to time—the Asiatic mode of production led to 'stagnation' once the rupture between Asia and Greece permitted the transition of the peasant commune to the city, and the city to the modern state.

Doubtless, 'do-gooders' were not lacking to 'cause the currently underdeveloped countries to believe that they were ready to accede to development' and that only European imperialism had prevented them. Those countries which have known the Asiatic mode of production, as defined by Marx, can certainly evolve, and, in particular, change their civilisation ('the history of Egypt from the time of the Pharaohs to that of the caliphs is the best example [of this]') without however changing their mode of production. It is none the less true that this economic and social regime is one which is characterised by immobility.[2] And in order to escape this, good will does not suffice. It is first necessary that it be analysed in all its aspects and all its sectors. It is necessary, in order to break a structure, to obey the laws of structuration and destructuration which may be at work within that structure.

Unfortunately, if anthropologists have rigorously described the various types of extant, concrete structures, or have defined abstract and precise schema of structures, they have neglected these processes of structuration and destructuration within these types or these schemas—those which alone permit us to proceed from structuralism to an applied anthropology.

We shall take up one of the rare examples in which, to our knowledge at least, we find a definition of a structure deriving from a process of structuration. This concerns feudalism. And we know how much feudalism—whether one takes it in its exact or in its derived sense—is considered as one of the greatest obstacles to the politics of development.

Feudalism, then, is generally defined by the historical conditions of its existence, or by its mode of production, or by its effects (economic and social), and by a certain number of traits, such as conquest (which gives power to a dominant clan), or serfdom (which replaces slavery) or by relationships of clientship and a domanial regime; or still again, by the contractual form of relations between men. . . . But we have also, from John Galtung, a structural definition of feudalism which will help us to advance to the solution of our problem.

(1) A structure is feudal when a great correspondence exists between the positions of individuals—that is to say, when (if one takes the various dimensions of status by which men may be classified—kinship, economic rewards, political power) there is a parallelism; the same people occupy the same positions—high, middle or low—in all three hierarchies. Non-feudal regimes are characterised, on the contrary, by a cross-distribution of statuses, for example, high educational level and low level of economic rewards, or low educational level and high rewards.

(2) In a feudal structure, social interaction occurs in terms of the sum of the positions an individual occupies in the different societal dimensions; it is maximal among those who occupy high positions across the board; it is minimal among those who occupy universally low positions; it is intermediate among highly and lowly placed individuals. In other words, and to take Galtung's exact expressions, the more central is the position of an individual in a communication network, the greater is the interaction between that individual and others having this central position. Conversely, those who are at the periphery—the serfs—interact little with each other; ultimately they are not allied one to another except by their common alliance with the lord, and in so far as they are exploited by those at the centre.

Thus, this structural definition postulates, in order to be understood, recourse to a preliminary process of structuring, which Lensky and Landecker have called 'status crystallisation'. What does this consist in? Crystallisation is the non-vertical dimension of social stratification which gives rise to phenomena of 'consistence' or of 'non-consistence' of social statuses, depending on whether or not it plays a role within stratification. There is consistence when diversified positions of individuals or of groups along diverse status dimensions align themselves; that is, when they are equally high or low. We have just seen that this is what defines feudalism.

But the phenomenon of crystallisation may be lesser—that is there may be societies with low consistence, where one individual or one group can have a high status in a certain dimension and a low status in another. Crystallisation certainly still acts in this case, but at a lower level. It is then, but only then, that what may be called 'questioners' of the social structure may appear. These will naturally be recruited not from among those who occupy a high position throughout, nor from those with a universally low one, but from among those who encounter barriers preventing them from crystallising their situation, or to their desire for high position at all levels, and along all dimensions.

Galtung emphasises these low levels of consistence in our contemporary societies, and draws from them a structural theory of aggression. We come to understand as well the importance of intellectuals in the context of 'questioners'. For though they have high status in the education dimension, they frequently have low status in the economic dimension, and with very rare exceptions, in the dimension of political power.[3]

It is easy to understand that a 'consistent' feudal regime presents a structure which is resistant to change, and that anthropologists cannot act upon it without acting on the formative process of crystallisation. We thus return to one of our previous conclusions—that concerning the primordial role of 'marginal men' in the social and economic development of their countries. The 'marginal man' but not the 'central' or 'peripheral' individual is significant. The peripheral individuals may certainly rebel momentarily, but will not become 'questioners' of the social structures by which they are bound. The importance of education, to the extent that it may be introduced into a feudal society, is that in creating a new status dimension—one based otherwise than on birth, economic rewards, or political power—it leads to the dis-organisation of the archaic consistence of the system, from within, and ineluctably and irreversibly to aggression all along the dynamic of change. The same is true of the appearance of new professions in towns, here again creating a new status dimension along lines of professional capacity, which is not consistent with the others. We have seen, in the chapter on acculturation in the Soviet satellite republics, the importance placed on this new working class, upon which the Russians relied to cause a break with Asiatic feudal forms.

Yet, two comments are necessary here. When we say that a process for change is introduced into a feudal society through the medium of least-crystallisation, this does not mean that from then on change operates peacefully, slowly, and without interruptions, since the group with maximal consistence will naturally defend its privileges against 'questioners' of the system. But violence will take the form of a directed struggle—thus creating a new structure —and not the form of savage rebellion, of the simple manifesta-tion of despair and poverty, which would underline the contradic-tions within the system but not abolish it.

Secondly, when we say that the struggle is 'directed' we are not saying that it is necessarily 'planned' and waged in the name of general values, transcending the group interests of the 'questioners'. In fact, to the extent that the countries of Latin America can be defined—if not as feudal in the medieval (European) sense of the term—at least as neo-feudal, the 'questioners' were actually re-cruited among the students of intellectual milieux on the one hand, and among the workers on the other. But the struggle was led, until very recently, in the urban context and not in the global one of the society, and it was more in the context of group interests than the common national good.

Unfortunately, structural analyses of this kind are rare. That which structuralism in general brings to applied anthropology— and we have alluded frequently to this—is the notion that the unity of a whole is not the simple sum of its parts; that the parts are dependent one on another and all depend in their turn on their gestalt formation. Further, that we must substitute for the old definition of social groups—in terms of the similarity of their members, the homogeneity of their values, and their common participation in the same collective representations (which can only yield us a classificatory science of groups)—a new definition, in terms of a whole set of relations, conflicts, cooperation, complementarity, hierarchy, which then permits us to proceed from a purely classificatory science to an 'operational' one. Operational because it is constructive, permitting us to introduce experimentation into social anthropology. As we see it, structuralism thus brings little to applied anthropology—a warning rather than a strategic possibility.

Given these conditions, it is understandable that the applied anthropologist prefers to structuralism—which, incorrectly, seems to offer the social engineer a mechanistic conception of the universe —a conception which, on the contrary, is probabilistic. He considers that structuralism, by insisting on the phenomena of self-regulation, homeostasis, and self-adaptation, can only ask of men that they bow gracefully to these 'mechanisms', and end in social conservatism, immobility and stagnation.

At the very least, if structuralism is obliged to leave a place for events, and for history, change may only be seen as spontaneous, interior to systems, and independent of human will. The probabilistic conception, which the upholders of applied anthropology accept, considers that if man cannot do everything, he may still do a great deal; he can invent 'possible' worlds which, through his action, become 'probable' worlds.[4]

In our view, this opposition to structuralism on the part of applied anthropologists is not valid except to the extent that one defines structuralism in terms of a conceptual schema, and within a rigid typology. It is not valid for those definitions of structuralism which seek, beneath equilibria, the processes of their formation and de-formation (like that of crystallisation). In the latter case, in effect, structuralism may be reconciled to probabilism, since it provides the means of possible manipulations for change. And that is why, even though brief, this chapter has seemed necessary.

NOTES

1. See, among others, L. Geertz (ed.), *Old Societies and New States*, The Free Press, Glencoe, 1963; *L'Afrique en devenir*, No. 13 of the review, *Prospectives*, Presses Universitaires de France, Paris, 1966.
2. The quotations in the paragraph are extracts from the article by G. Dhoquois, 'Les premières sociétés de classe. Les formes asiatiques', *L'Homme et la Société*, without our necessarily accepting all of that author's ideas.
3. On the whole of this analysis of feudalism and of status crystallisation, see G. Lensky, 'Status Crystallization, a Non-Vertical Dimension of Social Status', *Amer. Sociol. Rev.*, 1950; W. Landecker, 'Class Crystallization and Class Consciousness', idem, 1963; J. Galtung, 'A Structural Theory of Aggression', *Journ. of Peace Research*, 2, 1964.
4. W. G. Bennis, K. D. Benne and R. Chin, *The Planning of Change*, Holt, Rinehart & Winston, New York, 1961.

Applied Anthropology and Social Psychology

We must start with two points. First, if society is indeed made up of interrelated groups, these groups in their turn are made up of individuals who have desires, motivational powers or intentions of behaviour, impulses and dreams of the future, which may to a large extent be determined by the society in which they live, but which may also vary from one person to another. Behavioural similarity does not go so far as absolute homogeneity of persons.

Second, culture is not inherited as is instinct in a given animal species. Rather, it is learned, and is the fruit of education. This education, in general, consists in transmitting to the child the behavioural norms and the set of values of the global society in which he is to live. But then also, if the personality of an individual is in fact fashioned by his education, we may conclude that a different training will suffice to modify it.

A Chinese child taken at birth from his parents and raised by an American family will surely retain the distinguishing characteristics of his race. But psychologically, he will have an American sensibility, affectivity and mentality. These two points make possible a contribution by psychology to applied anthropology. We shall explore several of its contributions, those that seem most important, to see in what degree and to what extent we can integrate them into our purpose.

Admittedly, there exists a 'colonising' utilisation of data of human psychology rather than of scientific psychology within the framework of a development plan. We may take the example of the action of the former white colonisers in the Amazon territories. They began by giving gifts to the Indians, so as to instil in them new needs that could only be satisfied by manufactured goods. Then, when these needs had become demanding, they only continued to give the goods against payment. The Indians, having no cash, found themselves obliged to give their lands in exchange. Once deprived of their lands—from then on the property of the whites—they found themselves compelled by these same needs for manufactured goods to give their labour potential in exchange, and thus passed from liberty to servitude.[1]

Here, there is a somewhat diabolical use of a current and banal psychology of man as the being of desire, with a view toward a structural transformation of a society from a communal to a neo-feudal type, for the sole benefit of white colonists. In a less reprehensible form—since they may be used for collective progress as well as for the exclusive profit of one social class—the mass media are viewed as one of the most effective means for transforming a preindustrial into an industrial society, by raising the level of aspirations, by extolling a different life-style, and by diffusing European modes of existence.[2]

As an example of the use of scientific psychology toward the realisation of a plan, we can give Moreno's use of sociometrics to ensure the success of migratory movements. In Latin America, they have tried, for example, to get the Indians to leave the high plateaus, where they live poorly on barren land, for the Amazon forests, where they could turn to cash-crop cultivation. In Africa, they have projected the transfer of certain tribes from high density areas where resources are insufficient for the number of inhabitants, to regions of lower density with possibilities for more ample resources. In all these cases, ethnologists have been called in to show to what extent those populations which are to be displaced may agree to live near others. Moreno's sociometrics provides a number of tests that were proposed in the United States for the best possible distribution of migrants—Europeans and others—arriving to stay in America, so as to avoid forced colonisation and its ensuing tensions.

Of 250 families, a total of 125 is considered the maximum suitable for a projected community. The idea is that the selection should occur among the 250 families in such a way that the new community will resemble as closely as possible one which would have developed spontaneously if the people were free to choose, rather than being bound by development schemes. To this end, Moreno proposes the following tests for the population in question: 'What families (three to be listed in order of preference) would you choose to live with you in your new location?'; 'Whom would you choose to work with you in a given sort of job?'; 'List in order of preference three jobs you would like to have'; 'What families would you like to have as immediate neighbours? (three choices)'.

After six months of life in the new location, a second sociometric study should be carried out to see whether integration has been successfully achieved or, if not, to institute the necessary modifications. We know that Moreno contrasted this sociometrics with Marxian revolution, for he said, it is not enough to change infrastructures for people to be happy; it is also necessary that interpersonal relations be the expression, or crystallisation of human desires. They must be allowed to establish themselves spontaneously, and not under compulsion from the planner. In a word, there is a place for recognising micro-revolutions within or without a macro-revolution because they are more effective than it is.[3]

However, within this second trend—that of the use of scientific psychology—it is the methodology and group dynamics of Kurt Lewin that seem to have been most used by anthropologists, doubtless because Lewin's 'field theory' in social psychology greatly resembles the structuralist notion in anthropology. The 'field' integrates in a unique configuration cultural and historical elements (values, ideology, life-styles of individuals), sociological elements (structures of intra-group relations, rural or urban organisation), psychological elements (intelligence and personality of its members) and, finally, physical elements (race, health, geographical milieu) to create a topological space that defines all these elements by their interdependence within a single system. This notion of field, however, remains a static one. And we saw in the last chapter that applied anthropology takes a dim view of structuralism because of its too static and mechanistic aspects.

Group dynamics, though based on the same preliminary notion, takes us from equilibrium to change, without denying what the idea of fields contributed. That is, to change a social equilibrium, the totality of the field must be envisaged, including the groups and elements enveloped in it, their relations and mutual interdependence. The life of a 'group' is represented by a whole set of forces that ensure these relations and link sub-groups and individuals just as do those that are expressed in the creation of communication networks or their disruption. All of which means that our field finally depends on the ability of the planner to determine the different points of application of such forces as well as the direction of resulting forces. . . . To transform them, then, it is necessary either to create an additional force that will break old habits, or to diminish the force of the value conceded to certain elements of the pre-existing field.

According to Lewin then, to obtain a durable change, it is not enough to modify only the situation, or only the individuals. The whole social field in which individuals find themselves, and find themselves in certain situations, must be modified. If not, those forces interacting within it will sooner or later re-establish the former configuration.

The methodology, rendered very concise, will consist (1) in a knowledge of the strategic points of the field and (2) in a collective decision. Let us take an example from applied anthropology, that of the transformation of dietary habits of a given population. The first problem is how to proceed—by means of the press, of radio, or of printed notices. On whom to act—sellers of dietary products, housewives who do the shopping, children at school who eat in the cafeteria.

To answer this set of questions, the anthropologist begins with a series of soundings among the various levels of the population, so as to discover the 'forces' that act on dietary demands, and those that form 'barriers' to the purchase of certain specific products. This is what Lewin calls the search for strategic points by means of which anthropology may act on the field. But here, an authority system is powerless; the decision must be democratic and collective, that is, taken by those who are themselves concerned.

It is here that we reach the second phase: the utilisation of small groups of people won to the research, to whom the reasons operating in favour of a change have been explained, and who have accepted them. One does not attempt to transform the dietary system of the whole population at the first try, since one cannot succeed. It is necessary to use small groups of individuals who have received special training, and who then form—within the whole society—sorts of radioactive particles to provoke the collapse both of the old social situation—here the dietary one—and of individual attitudes that are topologically linked to it—here the habits of consumers.

It is to this formation of specialised and 'radioactive' groups that group dynamics is devoted, and it is based on the following principles:

(1) It is easier to change individuals in a group than when they are taken in isolation.

(2) Discussion in the group can create 'motives' for change among individuals, but a change in ideas will not necessarily be expressed in a change in behaviour. What group dynamics shows is that discussion changes the personality as it goes on; individuals are not the same after it as they were before. Briefly, group dynamics is not a simple exchange of words, but rather it is action.

(3) It is true that often the collective decision arrived at is not durable; the group may return from the level it has reached to the former one. All planning should thus take into account the problem of durability of the new level reached. But it seems that by giving a control group the thrilling task of changing the habits of the global society, one assures at least for that control group sufficient force for the preservation of this new level.[4]

These two examples suffice to show that in planning that seeks to base itself on multi-disciplinary action, the psychologist can provide a valuable contribution. Yet as we shall see, in the two cases of sociometrics and of group dynamics, micro-changes are at issue, or else it is a question of an equilibrium that remains limited to one sector of the society. The criticism that one can make of these two methods or techniques of action is thus the same as that which we have been led to make of American cultural applied anthropology, which is not concerned with solving the problem of change at the national level, but only at that of the peasant 'community' and sometimes even only the change of one or two culture traits within that community. We need not delay further here. But it is still useful to note in passing that psychologists should be included in the elaboration of planning projects, as well as in their realisation.

But this is not the object of this chapter. Rather, it is to see whether it is necessary to choose between an applied anthropology and an applied psychology. We certainly have to do here with two very different sciences, opposed in their principles as well as in their procedures. We must contrast them to see whether another type of relationship can be substituted for their present conflicting one.

We have already encountered this problem when, with Herskovits, we distinguished between acculturation—that is a facet of change—and enculturation—that is a facet of resistance to change. We have discussed acculturation in depth. So in this chapter we must turn to the nature and effects of enculturation, which is the process by which a culture, with its own behavioural norms and values, is transmitted by parents to their children.

This process is so important that it is always included in the very definition of culture. Linton, for example, says 'a culture is the configuration of learned behaviour and its results, whose compositional elements are transmitted by the members of a given society'. Or again, 'societies perpetuate themselves by teaching the members of each generation the cultural models appropriate to the positions they are supposed to occupy.' True, all individuals do not learn as children all these elements—especially when societies become more and more complex.

Linton distinguishes the 'universals' which are shared by all enculturated members, and the 'specialties' that vary according to the positions the members are meant to fill as adults—peasant, artisan, merchant, priest, etc. But even here, the determination of personality by society, of these 'statutory' and no longer 'ethnic' personalities, is a 'conserving' of the old culture. For these learned roles must be coherent with and complementary to each other, and must all be adapted within a configuration. 'All cultures include a solid nucleus, well-integrated and relatively stable, consisting in mutually adapted universals and specialties, and a fluid, little-integrated, constantly changing area of alternatives that surrounds this nucleus.' The area of change is thus fairly restricted, as may be seen.[5]

But Linton's definition is still ambiguous, and as a result, it may be accepted both by social psychology and by cultural anthropology. We must take a further step and distinguish two different types of learning—that of personality (that is, the set of learned culture traits) and that which results in a structuring of personality. Under the influence of Freudian psychoanalysis, anthropology was led to emphasise—with Ruth Benedict, Margaret Mead, and finally Kardiner—the process of personality formation of the adult during the first years of his life more than the process of learning culture traits. If the latter could be prolonged throughout life, any individual could acquire the patterns of another culture than his own at any point if he found this to be advantageous. The former—if we accept the views of Freud and his anthropologist disciples—is closed, and definitively closed, with the liquidation of the Oedipal phase. The personality structure cannot change after that. Thus, we have two possible definitions of enculturation—one of them broad, as for example, that of Spindler:

'Enculturation is the process by means of which the individual acquires the culture of his group, his class, his segment of his society . . . This process is limited to the acquisition of patterns of behaviour—including language, meta-languages, customs, values, role definitions, and other phenomena of the same order. Following the characteristics of this definition, one can place the accent either on the transmission of culture by cultural agents such as parents and teachers, or on its assimilation by the individual, including the response to a similar transmission.'[6]

The other definition, which is narrower, would be that of Herskovits: 'the enculturation of the individual in the first years of his life is the primary mechanism that creates cultural stability, while the same process when it operates on older people is especially important for induction to change.' But he adds, 'the enculturative experience in adult life, however, is only intermittent. It presents a striking contrast with the continuous conditioning to which the newly-born or the small infant is exposed. . . . For the adult, enculturation is terminated with the exception of cases in which he must react to new situations.' Finally, Herskovits emphasises the unconscious nature of this primary process, while the learning of borrowed culture traits is always conscious.[7]

It is clear that if we accept the second definition, culture is in some way misshapen, and we then understand not only phenomena of resistance to change, but also the distortions that operate in culture transfers, the facts of reinterpretation or of syncretism.

From that point, from these personalities culturally structured by their families, one understands as well why the new habits that acculturation has been able to create are hardly solid, and so often retreat before others—former habits which are strongly rooted in the unconscious, and which have been only provisionally suppressed.

Adams cites the case of a woman of a Guatemalan village who thought herself very modern and not superstitious (she did not believe in the evil-eye) and who, when her child got sick, had taken him to the doctor. Faced with the failure of scientific therapy, she returned to her former beliefs. The evil-eye existed and she must call the sorcerer-healer. We finally come to understand that when planners impose new habits on a population which contradict those formed in early childhood, feelings of anxiety will develop which may lead to neurosis or even to real psychosis. Concrete studies of acculturation in Africa provide many examples of this.

The conception of experimental psychology is completely different vis-à-vis the theory of learning. Here, the two key notions are those of gratification and punishment. The theory of learning is based on the existence of needs in the child, needs for nourishment, security, motion, etc. But each of these needs can be satisfied in a different way in accordance with cultural factors. Education consists in creating conditioned reflexes linking the satisfaction of each of these needs to a certain form of cultural behaviour. To create these reflexes, one 'gratifies' the child who follows the model transmitted by his parents; one 'punishes' the child who does not conform to it. In brief, enculturation consists in furnishing the institutionalised techniques of response to a given primary need so that its satisfaction occurs according to cultural models, so as to create secondary needs by a whole process of alternated reward and punishment.[8]

Following a similar perspective, the possibility of cultural change is—unlike in the preceding one—amply validated. For:

(1) Learning continues throughout life, and consequently, we proceed past the opposition enculturation-acculturation—the processes in the two cases do not vary.

(2) A cultural element can change each time the following psychological conditions are fulfilled: first, if in the society one wants to change there are needs that are not satisfied, or that are poorly satisfied. Further, the new solutions proposed to satisfy them are, naturally, understood, judged valid, and the models transmitted can be learned. Finally, these new behaviours give the satisfaction that the former culture could not give.

(3) Change does not occur apart from all situations of anxiety unless one introduces a gratification for the one who adopts it and a punishment for the one who refuses it. Thus, it will no longer be the change but, on the contrary, the perpetuation of former habits that will become traumatic, while the acceptance of the new becomes a source of gratification.

This is what psychologists call 'counter-conditioning'. For example, Adams recommends, as a plan for nutritional change among the peasantry of Guatemala—whose nutritional base is red beans—

to rely on the desire of the peasants to climb the social ladder, showing them that red beans are symbolic of the diet of the lower classes, and that if they continue to eat them, they will continue to have an inferior status within the society. In this way, change is rewarded by the sentiment of having risen to the style of life of the upper class; conservatism is punished by the sentiment of social failure.

(4) Social psychology, however, recognises the force of childhood habits, from which it is very difficult to detach people. The child is, on the other hand, malleable wax in the hands of educators, from which follows the importance given to the school. A case in point—to prevent action by the family that could counteract that of the teachers, there is a policy of putting the child into boarding school as early as possible. This was the policy of the Jesuits in Latin America, and of Protestant missionaries vis-à-vis the Indians on the reservations in the United States.

It was also, to a lesser extent, the policy of colonisers in Africa; it is that of independent (African) governments today. For these governments wish to industrialise their countries, and industrialisation is linked to the acquisition of a new mentality—the sense of assiduous work, punctuality, respect for discipline, and with that, a different conception of time from the one characteristic of peasant peoples.

I have read, in this connection, a very relevant report of an attempt at the amelioration of living conditions in an Indian community which was made by Catholic missionaries. It seemed to those who undertook this work that the state of poverty of these natives was such that it would be Pharasiacal to try to save their souls without first having brought relief to their bodies. The missionary work was provisionally set aside, and they concentrated on changing the nutritional system, the traditional treatment of illness, teaching them to build more hygienic houses, to improve local artisanry, etc. The effort was a total failure.

And so the missionaries perceived that all these material changes were products of a certain mentality, one opposed to the communal one of the Indians. It would be necessary first to give them a sense of individualism, of the dignity of the human person, to transfer discipline from the outside (social control) to the inside (moral law); in brief, they had followed the inverse path to the one they should have followed. They had put the cart before the horse, and the first and most urgent task was to Christianise them. That is, basically, to Westernise the Indians. The rest would follow abundantly and, so to speak, automatically.

We have then two conflicting conceptions, neither of which denies the possibility of innovation. But the anthropological one is more pessimistic, accenting resistance. The other is more optimistic, even too naively so, for the ethnologist. But the concern for the underdeveloped countries today is so great that we now see a rapprochement between these two points of view.

First, it is in terms of a redefinition by anthropologists of the concept of enculturation. Brameld finds that 'it is dangerous to introduce a gap between the old and more recent stages of encul-turation in the child,' for the child even in his first years does not passively receive that which comes from his parents—he re-thinks it, he chooses, he has a 'critical capacity'.[9]

Lifton, in the same way, supports the view that primary educa-tion includes a 'conscious enculturation', since the child is not only subjected to the influence of his parents, but also to that of his 'peers' and all the stimuli that come from the external environ-ment and to all the new models of conduct that enter into him. This means that, at least in societies in transition, two conditions of change appear—'psycho-historic dislocation' that destroys the old symbolic system, and 'image flux' brought about, for example, by the mass media, to build a new type of man, 'protean man', characterised by a perpetual transformation of himself—as opposed to the man definitively fixed in the congealed structure of his personality.[10]

Doubtless, it is important to recognise that in traditional societies, the process of enculturation is oriented toward the inter-nal, and relies on the imitation of adults, conformity, and identifi-cation. But more and more, to use Riesman's terms, the individual is 'other-directed', he takes his models from the external world and not only from the closed circle of the family.[11]

And elsewhere, as Wallace points out, even in societies that have remained traditional, there is a great diversity of personalities, which seems to prove that culture is not unconsciously transmitted and uniformly internalised; that the culture of personality is not the simple internalisation of the culture within which the personality is formed—that enculturation in childhood is not a unilineal but a multi-lineal process.[12] In consequence, a whole trend is beginning in the domain of anthropology, to limit the effects of an idea of enculturation as unconscious structuring of the human personality, in favour of the more psychological notion of 'personality dynamics'.[13]

For its part, development psychology is transforming itself. True, it still continues to affirm its 'primacy'. It always reproaches anthropology and sociology for trying to discover and apply general laws of the process of change without taking account of concrete circumstances, or fixing *a priori* the ideal level of modernity to be achieved, and of believing that one can abolish obstacles that retard modernisation by the mere introduction of foreign capital, experts or technicians, or the reform of institutions. All these measures have proved themselves inadequate up till now because even the elites of underdeveloped countries lack the necessary mentality for successful modernisation. What must be created first of all is a personality system capable of progress.[14] The psychological perspective thus retains all its interest. However, that perspective can, at least to a certain extent, yield a place to a conception of enculturation as the structuring of personality.

There is, for example, a whole 'logic of industrialisation' that is based on the establishment of an 'open society', one in which no obstacle—of an ethnic, religious, or secular nature—is opposed to geographical, professional and social mobility of individuals; in which statuses are achieved by capacity, not ascribed by birth. But the history of ethnography shows that this logic does not act exactly in the same way in the case of different types of societies or groups, e.g., dynastic, middle-class, colonial administrators, nationalist leaders; that there are thus several possible roads leading to the industrial society.[15] That is, the industrial society is not, properly speaking, a society at all—the term itself is false—but rather a cultural model. And naturally, this cultural model, to the extent that it is accepted, and where it is generalised from one society to another, will be expressed differently, according to the national character and the cultural heritage of the people undergoing industrialisation.

As a result, this model will certainly come from outside, but it comes as a set of new values, aspirations and behaviours acquired through acculturation and not as a 'structure'. On the contrary, it becomes structured according to national character, or according to what Kardiner called the 'base-personality', which is the product of enculturation.

Finally, and above all, the progress from the theory of learning to that of personality dynamics will permit an intimate meshing of contemporary psychology and anthropology, in the sense that it will allow the anthropologist to shade the concept of enculturation by giving greater place to individual reactions and conscious choice. At the same time, it will allow the psychologist to give proper place to the structuring effects of personality and to familial enculturation, alongside 'external' influences. For what defines personality dynamics is not the elements by which it is formed, in their chronological order, but the notion of continuous 'growth' and of gradual maturation starting from those elements. As a result, this dynamic is not enclosed in a definite structure, but it allows room for structural factors, from earliest childhood, in the play of its progressive development.

Contemporary psychology considers that the influence of the family is integrated into the ulterior development of personality; it does not disappear, but continues to be included in the dynamic —enriched, remodelled, and restructured in a different way. Applied anthropology may have need of psychology, but that psychology must be penetrated by ethnological knowledge. For the acceptance of change demands the action of the 'donor' alongside that of the 'recipient'. This recipient does not receive the new traits by reasoning as we do (at least according to the ethnocentrism of most international experts) but according to the cultural models of his own thought. Our two perspectives are thus reconciled.

One more comment must be added. The concept of personality dynamics should lead to a reform of the older psychology's theory of learning, with its use of reward and punishment. One has wanted to oppose familial enculturation by means of a school addressing itself to the malleable child, who was therefore manipulable, and on whom the teacher could act as the parents would act. One can ask oneself, in these circumstances, if the school does not then become formative of passive personalities. It certainly does not, since, as we have seen, the child reacts to the education of his parents. And he will also react to the instruction of his teachers. It is nonetheless true that the school is not necessarily an instrument of human liberation and of societal change—unless it changes pedagogically.

The old psychology of development contrasted two varieties of enculturation of the same kind—that of the domestic group and that of the school, the school having to triumph in the end. Frequently, it only created marginal men and developed what Herskovits, in *The Life of a Haitian Valley*, called 'socialised ambivalence'. The new psychology of development, based on personality dynamics, claims a dual change—of familial education and of schooling—destined not to create an adaptation to the surrounding cultural world in the case of the domestic group, or the adaptation to a new modern and progressive society for the instructing group —but to create a type of man capable of change, choice, development of self, and self-modification in modifying his own environment: a man capable of enriching and amplifying himself via exchange, cooperation, and opening toward others. Applied anthropology must not neglect the essential role of post-familial education, but it owes it to itself to propose a different 'anthropology of education' from that which the West has exported up till now, and which, in the final analysis, has become bankrupt.[16]

NOTES

1. Roberto Cardoso de Oliveira, *O Indio e o Mundo dos Brancos*, S. Paulo, 1964.
2. D. Lerner, *The Passing of Traditional Society*, The Free Press, Glencoe, 1958.
3. J. L. Moreno, *The Sociometry Reader*, The Free Press, Glencoe, 1960.
4. K. Lewin, *Field Theory in Social Science*, Tavistock Publications, London, 1952; *Resolving Social Conflicts*, Univ. of Michigan, Ann Arbor, 1948. Cf. also R. P. Girod, 'Les Théories et les Méthodes de Kurt Lewin', C.I.S., IX.
5. Ralph Linton, *The Study of Man*, D. Appleton-Century Co., New York, 1936; *The Cultural Background of Personality*, D. Appleton-Century, New York, 1945.
6. G. Spindler, 'Psychocultural Adaptation' in E. Norbeck *et al*, *The Study of Personality*, Holt, Rinehart & Winston, New York and London, 1968. Spindler prefers the term 'cultural transmission' or 'acquisition of culture' to that of enculturation (Beals, Spindler and Spindler, *Culture in Process*, Holt, Rinehart & Winston, New York, 1967.)
7. M. J. Herskovits, *Man and His Works*, Alfred Knopf, New York, 1948. Cf. M. Spiro, 'Culture and Personality: the Natural History of a False Dichotomy', *Psychiatry*, 14, 1951, pp. 19–46.
8. Cf. J. Dollard and N. E. Miller, *Social Learning and Imitation*, Yale College Institute of Human Relations, New Haven, 1941. For the application of this learning theory to applied anthropology, see R. N. Adams, *Introduccion a la Anthropologia Aplicada*, Guatemala, 1964.
9. T. Brameld, *Cultural Foundations of Education*, Harper & Bros., New York, 1957.
10. R. Lifton, 'Protean Man', *Partisan Review*, 1968.
11. D. Riesman, *The Lonely Crowd*, Yale Univ. Press, New Haven, 1961.
12. A. Wallace, *Culture and Personality*, New York, 1961.

13. In this paragraph we have summarised the ideas supported by Nobua Schimahara in 'Enculturation—a Reconsideration', *Current Anthropology*, April, 1970, pp. 143–234.

14. A. Gunder Frank, 'Sociology of Development and Underdevelopment of Sociology', op. cit.

15. C. Kerr, J. T. Dunlop, F. Harbison and C. Myers, *Industrialism and Industrial Man. The Problems of Labor and Management in Economic Growth*, Harvard Univ. Press, Cambridge, Mass., 1960.

16. T. Brameld, *The Remaking of a Culture—Life and Education in Puerto Rico*, Harper & Bros., New York, 1959: critique of the North American authoritarian type of pedagogy; apology for a pedagogy based on participation, dialogue for underdeveloped countries.

Here we must stop for a moment and glance back over the ground we have already covered. We have shown how and why applied anthropology appeared, though of course this is not to say that men have not always tried to manipulate each other—rhetoric and sophistry were born with the Greeks. Before that, and today as well, there have always been education and politics. That manipulation, however, remained empirical; rhetoric and sophistry are enumerations of the distortions of communication. Though they do postulate a certain conception of man, they do not formulate a real anthropology. Today, on the contrary, scholars wish to emerge from empiricism or the mere collection of facts, and to build a science of conscious and purposive manipulation of men and their societies, namely applied anthropology.

The growth from empiricism to science properly speaking has appeared as contemporaneous with that from what we have called 'free' to 'forced' acculturation. Free acculturation then belongs to history, not that the anthropologist cannot discover its laws, as we have seen. But these laws follow the random chance of events, and causes unfold the chain of their effects without our knowing where they will lead. The result is thus both determined—since there are laws—and contingent, since we let them proceed without taking account of them. Planned acculturation, on the other hand, lies in the realm of science, as defined by Bacon or Comte: 'to know is to foresee, so as to act.'

But to act for what, and toward what? From the beginning, we are hurled against the problem of ends. And, because we still retain the liberal conception of science, we have left the problem of ends aside. Since its birth, applied anthropology has belonged to the ideological context of democracy, of the hierarchisation of values, and of social pragmatism. But all the same, it was born at the moment when that ideology was breached by Marxism, Freudianism, and the sociology of knowledge. From whence derives its ambiguity—which we have tried to ignore throughout this work, because we have been outlining a new science in the process of its formation—but which now, stepping back, appears highlighted.

The liberal conception of science separates the realm of ends—which is left to philosophical speculation—and the knowledge of means, which belongs to science. Finally, then, applied anthropology is merged with general anthropology; it is the discovery of those laws that regulate the evolution of societies and their cultures. Once these are known, the scholar can foresee that a given cause will have a given effect, and insofar as this effect seems 'good' or 'useful', or 'bad' or 'noxious', he may either keep this cause from occurring, or he may provoke it, or finally, if he cannot keep it from occurring, he will control its course as much as possible.

There will then be on the one side an objective, impartial science, detached from all value judgements—a pure description of facts and the laws which govern them—and on the other, an 'art' that will consist in the application of this knowledge in terms of certain objectives, dictated 'from outside', and which are then, exterior to and transcendent over that knowledge—the political will of governments and preferences for given value systems. We have seen that there may be conflicts between the political objectives of administrators and the moral convictions of the social engineers on whom they call. The famous phrase of Lévy-Bruhl admirably defines this liberal period: 'there is a science of means, but no science of ends'.

Still, applied anthropology developed during an epistomological crisis, and was necessarily marked by it. And first, it was marked by the effects of Marxist and Freudian discoveries, and with them, the appearance of concepts of rationalisation, mystification, reification, and repression. No one could any longer consider

the scholar as 'free' or, if you prefer, as a being entirely dedicated
to the principle of reality escaping the impulses of his unconscious,
the interests of his social class, or of his ethnic group. The time is
past when Pasteur could say: 'when I enter my laboratory, I close
the door of my chapel.' The scholar enters his laboratory taking
with him his religious, political or economic 'chapel'.

Yet, if it is not easy, it is at least theoretically possible for a
scholar who sets the search for truth above all other values, to
fight against his 'ideologies,' using a preliminary consciousness of
his 'commitments,' a sort of preliminary psychoanalysis of his
intelligence. But we know that if the scholar is influenced by his
ideology, it is not manifest, but is the 'payee' of his personality and
his thought mechanisms. The scholar is 'programmed' like a
machine by the social and cultural milieu and he responds, in his
search for reality, only to the programme that has been given
him.[1]

But this is not all. We also know that human realities are of
another order than physical realities. Merton has shown the importance of the principle of recurrence which causes human nature to
become what we think it is. And so, we transform ourselves
according to the image we have of ourselves. And what is true of
the individual is also true of society; the principle of recurrence
is equally at play on that level.

It is sufficient to link these two statements—that the scholar is
always 'committed' whether he is aware of it or not, and that
there is an element of recurrence—for applied anthropology to
cease to be an art added to a science, to become itself an object of
scientific enquiry; the end is no longer separated from the means.
It is rather an integral part of action, and it must be understood
within the acculturative system. And this is just what we have been
led to do in distinguishing planned acculturation in capitalist countries from that planned differently in socialist countries.

We confront this ambiguity again and again, first in the very
vocabulary of the anthropologists we have cited. We sometimes
use the term 'process', as opposed to that of 'structure,' and sometimes the term *praxis* introduced by Marxism. This dual vocabulary

corresponds to a dual perspective; that is, our two types of planning correspond to two differing conceptions of science. The first, that which uses process to describe change phenomena, belongs to a causal or determinist perspective. The second, using the term *praxis*, belongs to a finalist perspective—one can only interpret human behaviour as a function of the 'direction' or 'intention' of that behaviour. Marxists claim that American anthropologists reify *praxis* in reducing it to a process and thus, dehumanising it. Just as bourgeois economists reduce to a 'relation between things' (exchange of one article for another) what is in fact 'a relation between people'.[2] So bourgeois anthropologists reduce to relations of laws what are relations between men.

But reciprocally, if we define planning action in terms of *praxis*, we are obliged to note (as we did in the chapter on Soviet acculturation) that there may be a gap between the effects or consequences of that *praxis* and its orientation or direction, and that gap will lead to the use of violence or force so that the results mould themselves to the ends. This ambiguity of vocabulary, then, well expresses a more basic ambiguity, that of human reality. We will see below that there is a methodology which will allow us to emerge from it. But for the moment, what concerns us is that the primacy given to process or to *praxis* is a supplementary proof, should we need one, that the scholar becomes, according to the political context, a machine programmed from outside. He will resolve problems posed to him in terms of the code dictated to him by the context in which he lives, either the code of process or that of *praxis*.

Secondly, we have encountered this ambiguity in the very mechanisms of planned change. These mechanisms are themselves dictated not so much by scientific reasons (greater chances of success) that are manifest, as by ideological reasons, those of latent and not expressed ideologies. Thus, American cultural anthropology proposes community development in the belief that a community that changes will be an example for neighbouring communities to copy, yielding micro-planning. It desires first to change values, since value changes will lead to a change of behavioural norms and finally, this normative change will lead to a transformation of social structures, toward their democratisation.

But who will fail to see—as did the young anthropologists we cited—that the global society remains untouched, that such change occurs within the conservation of the structures of the enveloping nation, to the greater profit of a single class than of the community as a whole. For in reality, everything is linked, and community development is no more than '*bricolage*', a 'miniaturisation' or 'fragmentation' of progress, leaving intact the curbing forces that come from external manipulatory centres.

On the other hand, Soviet applied anthropology and development sociology place the accent on transformations of the infrastructures of the global society, realising that culture—as an epiphenomenon, that is the world of values and norms—will be modified in parallel ways. But to do this, it is obliged to introduce dichotomies within communities, to rely on one class as against another, to create a revolutionary class. Consequently, it refuses to remove change from the context of the participation of all in a common labour.

We need not take sides. But what we wish to underline is that the very mechanisms of planned action do not depend on a judgement of reality, of their relative effectiveness, but upon the political commitment (ideological or unconscious) of planners. The two are allied in so far as they put the accent on the goals of productivity, of economic growth, of an individualist mentality—even for rural areas—and in neglecting to speak of dependence, imperialism, the political goals of the state affecting these changes, the struggle of great powers to assure the clienthood of subordinated states (which is to eliminate internal feudalism only to substitute for it another form of feudalism only named as such by its opponents).

We know that a certain segment of youth has risen against these ends, among the Soviets as well as among the capitalists, showing that there are other values—and as a result, another applied anthropology or development sociology—those of free speech, sexual freedom, mystical communion, and merrymaking . . .[3] Sociologists and anthropologists manipulate social realities for the profit of those who, at the outset, have already manipulated them, and who have themselves internalised the values that only express the interests of those who control the 'situational definition' in which scholars will be employed.

It is easy to denounce ideologies. But one only denounces them in terms of others. We have confronted applied anthropology with other disciplines, which claim precisely to have overcome the obstacles encountered by the former, e.g., the 'miniaturisation' of development is overcome by sociology, and the impossibility of changing institutions without first changing mentalities is overcome by psychology.

Let us comment in passing on their basic oppositions, since if they do not mutually correct each other and become complementary, the former expects all changes of institutions to lead to the appearance of a new personality type while the latter expects a whole re-education of personalities, which will lead to the possibility or the viability of new institutions. In any case, both presuppose an ideology—that of the value of autonomy as against alienation, and of creative freedom as against the static. The theory of personality dynamics is only the reflection of a certain world view and a view of ourselves that derives from Christianity, Western philosophy, and competitive capitalism, perhaps especially when it is used by the most bitter opponents of that capitalism. Development sociology is merely the latest expression of evolutionary theory (to the point where Soviet ethnologists are always referring to Morgan and where evolutionism, which seemed definitively condemned by American cultural anthropology, rises with Wright from its ashes) a theory which in turn was only a rationalisation of the anterior idea of progress, going back even as far as the myth of Prometheus.

We may be excused for having, in this chapter, emphasised ideologies, which often hide self-interested motivations but which, even aside from their manipulation by political factions, express an unscientific 'cosmology' and 'anthropology' invaded by the values of our own milieu. For ethnography has familiarised us with other cosmologies and 'anthropologies' than our own, among which one might choose according to his preferences but which are rationally all equally valid.

There is, for example, that of 'participation,' which bases man in nature, and reciprocally, nature in man, which extols instead of the 'break' between spirit and things, a continuity between all parts of the cosmos, including our own. Or there is that of the Melanesians Leinhardt studied in *Do Kamo*. Also, there is that of the exemplariness or of the imitation of gods that models human behaviour according to primordial myths, so that from the gesture of a man sowing seed to that of love-making, from that of the weaver to that of the blacksmith, individual behaviour recreates that of the creator ancestors, and is rooted in the metaphysical—such for example as that of the Dogon elucidated by Griaule and his followers.

Why prefer as the font of all the sciences we have reviewed, our conceptions of man and nature over those of other peoples to the point where we consider it our 'duty' to make them change? The Indian resists, either in retreating into the forest, losing himself among the vines and humid obscurity; or else he tries to escape the pressures of Western society in climbing ever higher into the Mexican mountains, so as to attain the desert heights where hunger and death await him, since they cannot be cultivated. They seem to tell us, following the phrase of the Gospel, 'what doth it profit a man if he gain the whole world and lose his own soul?'

In the same way, ethnography proves that there are several ways of reasoning and that our rationalism is not the only valid use of reason. Alongside our thought, in terms of arbitrary 'signs', there is thought in terms of physical 'symbols'; alongside our reasoning by 'clustering' concepts (as Piaget so well defines it) there is another reasoning by 'correspondences' that permits us to pass from one stratum of reality to another, without enclosing them in more or less extended moulds. There is even a logic (it would be better to say several 'logics') of divination that proves the extreme plasticity of forms of thought and of the human mind.

If a certain use of reason—our own—allows us better to control nature so as to subject it to our desires, that does not mean that other usages do not have value, such as that of the inductive reasoning of divination to 'secure' man and render him apt for action in certain circumstances; for the need for security is a highly human one. As for reasoning by analogy, which is the basis of all systems of correspondences, it has always shown itself, in contrast to the scholastic system of clustering of concepts, to be the preferred type for scientific discovery and the generalisation from one sphere of reality to another of laws first found in the former.

However, contacts have been established between the West and non-Western peoples. Certain of the latter have already lost a great measure of their values, and have acquired new needs. Applied anthropology thus retains its validity, on the condition that it guards against itself, and remains always capable of self-criticism. We can now continue along our way, after this pause which at first seemed likely to be discouraging.

*　　*　　*

Doubtless, what has hampered us most in the first part of this book has been less the positive side of the issue—the existence of certain tendential laws in the realm of acculturation, permitting a manipulation of reality—than the negative, the existence of obstacles to change. It is these obstacles that led us to compare applied anthropology with related disciplines, without however having thereby overcome the difficulty. So we must now consider the reason for these obstacles.

Basically, the discovery of tendential laws was much more the work of general than of applied anthropology. The former followed the old conception of the role of science, that is to describe and understand facts. The latter took up the new conception of science, the one first proposed by Feuerbach among others when he said: 'philosophers have merely interpreted the world in different ways; what matters is to change it.' Manipulation of reality was, from then on, to take over from explanation and, naturally, not only the manipulation of physical reality but also, and especially, that of human and social reality. A manipulation then that could go, and manifestly did go, as far as the paradox of educating man for liberty by objectifying him, that is by considering him, when a child, as wax to be moulded.

Marx follows on Feuerbach. But Marx did not wish to base *praxis* other than on a scientific-type objectivity, and to model it on a truth exterior to action. That is to say, while emphasising the necessity for reversing the goal of science—from explanation to action—he by no means considered himself an all-powerful thaumaturge. He remained faithful to the old methodology, even though he surpassed it. Action must always submit itself to the criteria of experimental verification.

Closer to our own subject, Rauh supported an analogous ideal of morality when he defended the necessity of first observing practical realities, to see what in them is in contradiction to ethical values. Then, from these observations, it is necessary to formulate actional hypotheses to undertake to ameliorate that reality, and render it more adequate to moral norms. Finally, these hypotheses must be verified experimentally (creation of cooperatives, proposals of new laws, etc.) in submitting them to factual control. In both cases, then, the possibility of obstacles is recognised, but these obstacles are integrated into action.

Unfortunately, the extraordinary successes of physics, like the splitting of the atom, or of biology, to the extent that it is on the way to recreating original life forms, have led scholars who work in the human and social sciences to hope to achieve similar metamorphoses. From *praxis* submitting itself to experimental verification, we have passed to the thaumaturgy of man-the-god. It is true, and we must stop to emphasise this as well, that cultural anthropology tried to justify this transition. What does it say concerning it?

First, culture is not the result of nature; it even goes against nature, since it begins with rules—artificial or conventional rules that will direct human conduct. Culture is added to nature; that is why, though there is only one nature, there may nevertheless be so many cultures which differ so widely from each other. In brief, culture is the creation of man in society.

Second, man creates himself in creating his cultural works, since his personality is the reflection of primary institutions that he himself has 'institutionalised' through time. To a certain degree, anthropologists here rejoin the young Marx, without really knowing him, even while thinking themselves the opponents of Marxism.

What conclusion could applied anthropology, at the time of its formation, draw from these two statements? First, since all culture is a human creation, it is always possible to create new cultures, considered to be better than those already institutionalised. Second, that men will change at the same time that they change their cultures, that new types of men are forged in action. We do not say that these conclusions, and especially not the second, were explicitly drawn by American anthropologists, or that they are manifest in applied anthropology. But they remain adjacent, like the dynamic of a dream in its projects.

The result of this whole set of converging currents led finally to making politics the basic science (with which we think many young people will agree) beside which all the others can only exist as satellites. Marcel Mauss, without pursuing this idea to the end, had already perceived it when he crowned the set of sociological and anthropological sciences with politics, charged with giving the final ends for collective action. He did not proceed to the end, since he knew that not all ends are realisable. But he was interested in the Russian Revolution precisely because he saw it as an experimental laboratory, where one was experimenting with new social hypotheses—the elimination of cash, of the 'bourgeois' family structure, to take only these two examples. That is, he was interested in discovering the limits of politics, after having placed it as the crowning human science.

We have witnessed in the course of our life this broadening emergence of politics—for the author's youth was lived under the sign of the battle between Maurras, who proclaimed 'politics first', and the Marxist revolutionaries, who affirmed 'economics first'. And it is the sons or grandsons of these revolutionaries who today discover that it is not enough to change the system of production to transform culture, and with it man, and who now uphold the primacy of politics. We agree, but in faithfulness to the thought of Mauss—that is, that the primacy of politics should recognise the limits of the politic.

If one prefers, and to remain in our realm of applied anthropology, the existence of obstacles to development should not be seen as a provisional contradiction to the postulate of general anthropology that culture is a creation of man and that, because it is his work, it can be changed. The obstacles are then never insurmountable. It is necessary to integrate applied anthropology, as is shown by a revolt of determinism against all action that does not take it into account. We started at the beginning of this book with the existence of a determinism, that which assures us of the very possibility of the application of anthropology to the transformation of the world. We must now return to it, since this determinism also marks the limits of possible variation.

The first limit is that man is dual, and that if he is cultural, he is also natural. So, is everything biologically possible to him? In what measure does nature obey the norms of society and culture? It is useless, now when so much is being said about the environment, to belabour this point. Man is realising that by modifying the ecological conditions of his existence, he is in the process of signing his own death warrant. Pollution of the atmosphere, by atomic fall-out, but also by the development of atomic-powered industry; by the fumes from cars, from heating gas; pollution of the waters, of rivers and the ocean by industrial waste; disappearance of plant species and animals before our own disappearance; adulterated food . . . And against all these toxins, there is only a low-profile policy, so as not to effect the values of our ever more urban and industrial civilisation: control of gas leaks, treatment of waters given off by some factories, parks for a month's mandatory vacation . . . ! As though all the elements of life do not form a biological system that must remain balanced for the elements to survive.

Ricoeur characterises the current attitude with the term 'endless desire' in the sense of continual desire, and of unlimited augmentation of power left to its own dynamism and direction. The first trait 'manifests the derisory attitude of the society of production' abandoned to its lust. As for the second, it would reduce the world of man to 'the universal reign of the manipulable'.

This problem of ends—and thus that of policy—is well posed by this collection of pollutions, but as Ricoeur notes, so is the problem of biological determinism, which surpasses that of political solutions (control of technology, socialism with a human face): 'it is perfectly possible that an unlimited growth violates laws that we do not know of, and exceeds thresholds of tolerance of which we are unaware. . . . The denaturalisation of nature occurs within nature, and not everything is possible in nature.'[4] We are thus led back to discover the wisdom of the peasant, who does not direct the rain, heat, wind and dryness, and who knows the limits of his possible action in controlling the forces that surround him. Or that of those exotic societies whom we teach—under the pretext of productivity—to level their soil more rapidly and to modify the water balance by destroying forests to develop plantations for cash-crops.

But if everything is not possible in nature—and in man in so far as he is part of nature—will not things reverse themselves in the cultural realm? Let us accept, to begin with, that culture, as cultural anthropology proclaims, is entirely the work of man. It is no less true that man puts himself into his works, via his two main faculties—imagination and memory. We will stay with these two for the moment, for it is they that are operative at the stage we have now reached. Imagination is what permits change, and the faculty that envisages future worlds and then tries to realise them. In each century, with its mutations of infrastructures, which are always traumatic because of their *unexpected* effects, imagination is validated; utopia becomes a way of thinking—yesterday romanticism, and today, a return to the imaginary.

But man also has memory, we must not forget. That is, he is fashioned by the past and he cannot escape the control that the latter exerts on him. The piece of paper that has been folded retains the trace of the fold. The body that has been accustomed to a certain environment cannot manage to live in another without the risk of more or less serious physiological difficulties, if not death. The mind, too, carries within itself not only acquired habits, but also all the dead that went before us, and who continue to command us, to direct us along certain paths, and not others— those dead whom we would like to forget, in the conceit of our thaumaturgic epoch, but who, Comte recognised, remain infinitely more alive than we: 'humanity is peopled with more of the dead than of the living.' Doubtless, there are social and cultural muta- tions, but they do not occur just anyhow; they follow a certain inherited dynamic, that channels them. Without doubt, there are changes that may be the work of men (if there were not, we would naturally not have written this book). But these changes to succeed must follow what anthropologists call a cultural 'trend', that is, they must take the direction which the ancestors have already established.

A propos the Paris Commune, Engels speaks of a 'social un- consciousness', meaning that the collective creative experience en- genders the new without preconceptions. The protagonists of action are unaware of what they are really doing. In our opinion, this is one of the greatest of Engels' discoveries, and parenthetic- ally, another reason to mistrust planning and the belief that change obeys the programmes of rationalism.

But this is not the point that concerns us here. It is rather that there is another 'social unconsciousness', namely the unheard words of the dead in the discourse of the living. We are not thinking of what anthropologists call tradition, for tradition is conscious, formed by a set of perceived values and ideals, just as a revolu- tionary projection is conscious, made up of value-aspirations and projective-ideals. Engels does not speak of revolutionary projects; he speaks of social unconsciousness. Nor are we talking about tradition as a simple conglomeration of habits, which are certainly difficult to change, especially after a certain age, but on which one can always act, particularly when, as among the young, they are not yet crystallised and hardened.

We are speaking of a social unconsciousness, which is a structur- ing, an orientation, a trend in a certain cultural direction. It is not a simple repetition of actions from one generation to another through family teaching. For then there would be stasis. It is determinism unrealised and unformulated by the cultural dynamic, or to be clearer, the determinism of lines of innovation.

An applied anthropology that would substitute imitation for innovation—cultural diffusion for cultural dynamics—to bring to underdeveloped peoples the heritage of the Western dead, to replace that of their ancestors, to exchange their culture heroes (e.g., the Ashanti Spider or the Dogon Smith) for an imported one (e.g., Oedipus or Prometheus) will obviously encounter obstacles. And these obstacles do not come from men, but from what men have subjected to the laws of memory. Those who manipulate cultures in the name of values they believe to be general to all men, when they are in fact only their own ethnocentric morals, will then always face limits on their action. Alongside those limits that stem from the laws of nature or ecology, there are also those inherent in the very existence of concrete cultures, which makes them continuing realities, even in their apparent discontinuity.

We must go even further. We devoted a chapter to the relationship between structuralism and applied anthropology. There we took the term 'structuralism' in its most general sense, and not in the very specific sense given it by Lévi-Strauss. So now we must say something about Lévi-Straussian structuralism. It is impossible in a few words to define the thought of this author without caricaturing it, all the more because it changes and deepens throughout its development. Perhaps we shall even be arresting it at a point it has already surpassed.

What is important for us to note is that an identical system of laws explains the structure of language and meta-languages (as myths are), kinship systems, and cybernetic organisation, the rules of exchange among men and the mathematical laws of information theory. In short, cultural works—like the sciences of the cosmos—being the creations of mind, one necessarily finds in them the 'scar'—to use the Lévi-Strauss expression—left by their excision from the mind. To give a Kantian rendering of this structuralism, we would say that, for Kant as well, there are forms that exist *a priori*: forms of sensibility, and categories of 'blind' understanding.

For it is impossible to be conscious of them directly, and they rely on external data for structuring. And so it is for Lévi-Strauss. There is no difference between 'evolved' and 'savage' thought; they obey the same logical laws, and these logical laws impose themselves on all man's creation in such a way that these creations are structured by them.

If the problem of mythologies does not interest us here, that of the elementary structures of kinship must detain us a moment. From ethnographic descriptions we are familiar with several hundred alliance and kinship systems, but all these systems can be related, thanks to permutations among their elements, to two broad variables—restricted alliance and extended alliance. This last in turn points the way to marriage by payment and to Western marriage. Lévi-Strauss shows that the choice of partners—e.g., of patrilineal or matrilineal cross-cousins—'opens' or 'blocks' social links, that is to say, there are conditions of social existence which, if they are not respected, prevent all social life. We do not know whether we can here use the term 'determinism,' which has a very precise meaning. It is more a question of formal and logical conditions of the possibility of functioning, and even of the existence of a society. If not determinism, it is then at least a matter of the determining of cultural structures by mental structures.

This observation does not prevent the development of societies and their passing from one structure to another.[5] All that is attested is that the new structures that will appear—either spontaneously, by the effect of internal causes, or artificially, by the application of an exogenous model—will obey the same logical laws as did the former ones; and that it will always be possible to pass after the fact from one to the other by a system of permutations.

But if an applied anthropology is possible, given a similar perspective, it is still true that it touches the limits of the imaginary. Just as with Kant, at least in the context of pure theoretical reason, we can only know phenomena, not numena, so in this structuralism, there is a logic of creative *praxis* to which despite oneself, one is obliged to submit; one cannot remake man in that he is a system of *a priori* categories.

What emerges from this whole series of comments is that ob-stacles to development need not be imputed to superstition, to the privileges of political leaders, to ignorance, or to a pathological attachment to values which are seen by the social engineer as without real value, or as counter-values. Not that these types of obstacles do not exist. But there are also obstacles inherent in development itself, integrated within change; determinisms that mark the 'finalitude' of our action. True, man can always rebel against these laws, but the laws will then turn against him to destroy him. It is in this perspective that we must envisage applied anthropology:

—possibility of change;
—existence of multiple determinisms—ecological, sociological, psychic.

NOTES

1. We borrow this expression 'programming' from a recent article by D. Ingleby, 'Ideology and the Human Sciences', *The Human Context*, II, 2, London, 1970, pp. 159–87, which shows well the transfer of political action on men from the manifest (ideology) to the latent (mentality).
2. Lenin, cited by D. Ingleby, op. cit.
3. E. Morin, *L'Esprit du Temps*, Grasset, Paris, 1962.
4. Articles by R. Simon ('Le ver dans le fruit?') and P. Ricoeur (Vers une éthique de la finitude') in *Christianisme Sociale*, 7–8, 1970, pp. 383–91 and 393–5.
5. Lévi-Strauss affirms this clearly: 'If it is true, as we believe, that social anthropology obeys a dual motivation—retrospective and prospective—to the extent that being aware of an evolution into which rhythm inserts itself . . . we seek to validate our-selves by resembling those who went before us . . . just as a part of us continues to remain . . .; if it were expected . . . of the anthropologist that he presage the future of humanity, doubt-less he would conceive it on the model of an integration progres-

sively unifying the characteristics pertinent to quick and dead societies. The conversion of a type of civilisation which long ago inaugurated the historic future (but at the price of transforming men into machines) into ideal civilisation that would succeed in transforming machines into men.' Then, culture having been given the task of manufacturing progress, society would no longer be constrained to enslave men. 'Henceforth, history would develop on its own, alone, and society, placed outside and below history, could . . . assure that regular and almost crystalline structure which the best-preserved of primitive societies teach us does not contradict humanity. . . . In this perhaps utopian perspective, social anthropology would find its highest justification, since the forms of life and of thought that its studies would no longer have only an historical and comparative interest; they would correspond to a permanent good fortune for man.' (Le Problème de l'invariance en anthropologie', *Diogène*, 31, 1966, pp. 23–33.)

Applied Anthropology as a Theoretical Science of Practice

12

The observations we have just made remove us equally far from two possible conceptions of applied anthropology:

(1) The 'liberal' conception, so termed because of the period in which it became prominent, which distinguishes science—objective, disinterested, concerned to describe facts apart from value judgements—and art, which on the other hand is always oriented by values, and has as its goal the realisation of certain ends, but which to reach them relies on preliminary knowledge furnished by science. According to this conception, only general anthropology deserves to be called a 'scientific discipline'; applied anthropology can only be an art at the service of politics (as it was, for example for Malinowski, at the service of British colonial policy). It is a 'rational' art, certainly, and no longer an empirical one, but still an art.

(2) The more modern conception that we have drawn from Marxism, which links thought to action. The truth is not that which is, but that which we do. Reality judgements cannot be separated from value judgements. Besides, it is enough for us to think of a situation for us already to begin to transform it. According to this new conception, applied anthropology itself becomes a science; it is the science of reforming or revolutionary *praxis*. The mistake of this conception lies not in its principles but, as we have said, in its drawing away from Marx, who would accommodate *praxis* with the existence of scientific laws. A further mistake is its imagining that if there are obstacles to planning, they can be overcome or averted when actually it is really necessary for us to integrate at least certain of them into applied anthropology, as the rebellion of facts against their manipulators.

We are thus led to defend a third conception of applied anthropology, which sees in it—as does the second of the above two conceptions—a science and not an art, but here resembling the first conception—a theoretical science, even though it concerns practice, and one whose policy would be to develop an art later on, but which still can in no way be identified with art.

Before going on to defend this conception and justify it, we will refer to a certain number of neighbouring realms in which analogous if not identical conceptions have come to light.

Medical research, as defined by Claude Bernard, is a science and the practice of the general practitioner or specialist is considered as an art, if we think in terms of contrasting polarities. Still, there exists a region between the two, that of clinical research in which —according to Leighton—medical practice and scientific research are combined, the clinic allowing testing of results found in labs, and the use of 'human experimentation'. We know that the preponderence of our basic knowledge of cerebral functioning, for example, has been drawn from observations of cranial accidents, and from experiments carried out in the course of their treatment.[1]

Economics leads us to an analogous conclusion. In marginalist theory, the market appeared as an ineluctable given of the mechanism of the distribution of goods. The economist's goal then consisted in describing and explaining it. However, market planning with regard to nationalising the economy within a certain political and social context made the economist reconsider the marginalist notion. For it brought him new data undoubtedly furnished by political practice—but that were nonetheless objective facts, and thus scientific.

In the first place the market, from 'substance' became 'function', the function of the social context in which it is institutionalised. In the second place, marginalism started from micro-economics and proceeded to macro-economics by progressive generalisations. Planning, by immediately putting the economist in the realm of macro-economics, led him to observe that the laws of the latter are not a simple generalisation of the laws of the former. Rather, they are something else, something new that must be studied scientifically. Finally, it forced the economist to proceed from *homo oeconomicus*, which was formerly his only proper object of study, to *homo aleator et moderator rerum*. That is, to abandon old mathematics, powerless in this new terrain, to discover a new mathematical style, which begins with econometrics, and which is a mathematics of quality and no longer of quantity.[2] In other words, market planning allowed economics, through new and unexpected data supplied by it, to make new progress and to correct mistakes while remaining a science and not at all an art; a theoretical science of practice not a science applied to practice.

In psychology, group dynamics similarly causes a bridging of the gap between research and social practice. It has gone so far in this direction that the researcher renounces the right the former psychologist had to direct research; he can only sum it up and formulate the point that has been reached, if he is asked to do so. But he allows the research to take its own course; the action speaks and is not, by definition, directed. This leads to the joining of research and practice within the group which corresponds to a joining at the psychological level within the members who are interacting and, more especially, within the researching practitioner. Research and practice become one, the practitioner provoking change in the object he studies, but retaining his intellectual lucidity to the extent that he observes the others without participating in their search for group formation, and analyses the change caused by their encounters.[3]

This group dynamics brings us even closer to applied anthropology than does the physician's clinical research or market economics. First, because the researcher-practitioner is in the group, and his mere presence, even if he does not intervene to direct the discussion, is itself an instrument of modification of reality, as is also true of the presence of the ethnologist in an exotic society.

Secondly, it is nearer because the change itself provokes feelings of anxiety among the group's members, against which they react by various defence mechanisms, and because one can establish a parallel between these defence mechanisms on the one hand and, on the other, the resistance mechanisms to planning which we have found in our investigation of applied anthropology.

But naturally, it is applied sociology that can provide us with the closest models, those which we plan to discuss in this chapter. Fernandes distinguishes three stages in his formulation:[4] a first stage is that of the liberal era, of 'social work' which starts from the existence of pathological phenomena like riots, a rising divorce rate, or rising juvenile delinquency, and thus starts from the observation of facts and not from a wish to change them. It proceeds, by an investigation of the factors that led to the crisis, to discover their causes so as to be able later to eliminate the elements that have brought about social disequilibrium or abnormality of collective behaviour.

In the second stage, applied sociology recognises that if it is indeed necessary to fight against crisis situations, applied sociology cannot reduce itself to being a supplement to social pathology, for it is directed toward the future, and takes as its essential objective the intervention of reason as a social process. It 'recognises as historically valid' the will of man to transform existing social structures by 'giving them one direction or another.'[5]

But Freyer in his work confuses rational intervention with political action on the pretext that it is politicians that direct structural change (or that political pressure groups such as unions do). On the other hand, he thinks that sociological knowledge can transform itself into social force. Thus, he remains in favour of an applied sociology of the same sort as the applied anthropology we condemned in the last chapter since politics cannot do everything; there are laws of change and concrete conditions to be respected for structural transformations to be able to succeed. The thaumaturgic will of man has its limits.

In the third stage, there is Mannheim.[6] This desire on man's part to change things is taken as a fact. But, like all facts, it must obey laws, and applied sociology should be precisely the search for these laws. The old sociology asked the scholar to study the social object as a natural one (Durkheim said 'as a thing') and not to study the artificial alterations that this object could be made to undergo— the way in which man 'domesticates' the various elements of the social sector in which he lives when they do not appear to meet his ends. The new sociology must extend its investigation to the processes that unfold under the influx of social changes deliberately provoked by planners. True, these voluntary and rational interventions are opposed to the spontaneous changes that the old sociology studied. This does not mean that they cannot be studied scientifically, like all the others, by empirical and inductive methods.

The difference between this last conception of applied sociology and the first two is clear. Doubtless Mannheim does not deny (rather he emphasises) that such a science has a great practical interest. But it constitutes a theoretical and not a practical science, the science of the control of the social milieu, its laws and boundaries, by man. If it interests itself only in the conscious and rational action of men, it further interests itself in it only in terms of science, and following the rules of the scientific method. Perhaps it is in this current of ideas that one can place the actional sociology of Parsons, and more definitely that of Touraine in France. It is no longer a matter of considering applied sociology as a science of means with practice in view, but to make the practice of these means the object of a new, autonomous science—of a specialised branch of general and theoretical sociology.

Let us say in passing that this change of perspective also allows a revision of the sociology of education, which has such an important place in the preoccupations of our contemporaries just as it had an important place at the beginning of the nineteenth century: 'Open a school' said Victor Hugo, 'and you close a prison.' For we cling to the illusion that education can confer a capacity to modify human reality and social reality. True, today we give education new ends—to broaden the horizons of the masses, and no longer to adapt them better to the existing society.

We are elaborating a pedagogy of autonomy, of creative freedom, and not of the simple transmission of knowledge. We are trying to give education a greater elasticity in the realm of its operations vis-à-vis the pressures of the surrounding society. But it is also necessary to study this new education scientifically, to consider it as an experiment and not as an end in it.elf from which we hope to get a transformation of society and of culture, and thus the creation of a new type of man. Or, if you prefer, we must consider it as an hypothesis that must be submitted to verification and, as a result, must be objectively analysed in its processes and its unfolding.

In these two cases—the sociology of planning and the sociology of education—it is necessary, as Fernandes notes, to pay attention not to project actional interests on to theory (the latter should start from the sole observation of the facts of change and be only the sociological study of man's intervention in nature) nor to the preoccupations of theory about action. (The latter should be allowed all its liberty so that it can pose new problems, lead to the discovery of new laws, and in sum enlarge the sphere of knowledge from the study of social objects to that of the processes of alteration of these objects by and in practice, in so far as our practice invents new fields or new processes for action.)

*   *   *

We wish to propose a conception of applied anthropology related to the various disciplines we have enumerated. That is, as a scientific discipline separated theoretically from general anthropology and practically from the techniques of planned acculturation. One whose object would be the theoretical and not the practical understanding of the alteration of cultures and of societies by ethnologist-planners and anthropologist-practitioners.

Certainly, the problem of reconciliation between pure research and applied research more and more preoccupies the international scientific community. But the solutions that are proposed are distinguishable from those we shall defend here. It is a question here—and we do not in any way contest either its interest or its necessity—of overtaking pure or basic research, in which the scientific interest is dominant, and on the other hand, applied research in which the interest of the user is dominant, to establish a relationship of cooperation between the two, in a common research—that is to say, an operational or directed one. We then continue, according to this perspective, to distinguish between the two, since we make of applied anthropology a basic science; the study of the 'action' of men on nature, the search for its laws, processes of action, and its limits. This point is too important for us not to emphasise it a bit.

The progression of social science from factorial analysis to the building of systems—whose products are not the mere sum of their composite parts, but which must be treated from a global point of view—has allowed the elaboration, alongside basic research and applied research, of another type of research which is called 'operational'.

'Operational research has as its object the attack on a current problem of events, but neither includes nor implies experimentation. This type of research is characterised by its strategy and its methods. Generally speaking, these comprise the following phases: (a) observation of the "mission" of the enterprise; (b) identification of its objectives;[7] (c) establishment of criteria of realisation of these objectives; (d) elaboration of a system of measures for the evaluation—as a function of these criteria—of results obtained; (e) effective measurement of results obtained, and their comparison with the objectives; (f) closing of the feedback loop by establishing a relationship between the extent to which the objectives have not been met and what has been accomplished.'[8]

Operational research can propose a programme of action and in fact it always ends by making recommendations. However, this is only one element of the 'strategy' of research geared to action, and if action follows and does not succeed, the failure will not be due to the 'model' elaborated; one will then speak of 'resistance to change'. In fact, in operational research as in all research carried out in terms of action, one operates within a theoretical framework. One first provides a series of data that is transformed into a programme for action. It is, however, distinguished from actional research in the sense that it then follows up the application of the programme to 'evaluate' the gap between the objectives envisaged and the results obtained.

But, as its partisans stress, it is still not an experiment, and still less what physicists call 'an experiment to see'; what is evaluated is in effect the value of the 'system'. One does not at all study the action of man on social nature as 'mutational action'. We readily admit that what is tested in such research is the gap between the logic of mind and the logic of things; between scientific reasoning that has its norms and laws, and social life, which obeys other determinisms than those of reason. This is why, if the failure or at least the limited success of the operational model is proved, one will speak of 'resistance to change' as an external obstacle. The obstacle will not be integrated into the action.

There is another aspect in terms of which operational research is distinguishable from our applied anthropology. Operational research is the work of the scholar, of the social science specialist who, as we have said, only follows the rules of the scientific method, putting axiological values in parentheses. It leaves to politics, to the administrator and the social engineer the responsibility of developing a practical procedure from it. There is indeed cooperation between the one who produces the programme and the one who uses it, but in terms of a given division of labour. The liaison between basic and applied research is certainly established, through the intermediary of the transformation of the goal into quantifiable objectives, by the evaluation of relationships between both planned and achieved objectives. But one does not evade the theoretical-practical distinction, which is maintained.

It is on the contrary the action of the practitioner that interests us, no matter what his programme may be, and no matter the intellectual 'operations' that have preceded it. In other words, it is the manipulative action of 'experimental' research, and not of 'rational' research that is the objective we propose for applied anthropology. And as we have just said, according to the view of all its initiates, operational research is not 'experimentation', but only 'a research appropriate to the elaboration of policy'.

Two examples should help to clarify this difference of perspective.

There may be non-operational research that makes possible the elaboration of policy; and there is operational research that does not result in policy. We take our two examples from the great problem of race relations between blacks and whites in the United States.

An example of the first sort of case is the research carried out by Myrdal on the position of negroes in the US, which is not operational research and does not give directives for action. It is a detailed analysis, sphere by sphere, of the 'marginalisation' of men of colour and their non-integration; in sum, of their peripheral position vis-à-vis white society. It resulted in the observation that this position was in flagrant contradiction of the moral and political ideals of North Americans. Certainly, one finds in the Appendices of *An American Dilemma* analyses of action which are more interesting for applied anthropology as we conceive it than for operational research, e.g., the analysis of the 'snowball effect'. Nonetheless, this research of Myrdal's was the point of departure for favourable changes in race relations.

An example of the second sort of case is the following: Orlans reports that he did not find convincing evidence of the use, by federal departments in charge of national planning, of the social research studies they themselves sponsored, with the exception of the National Institute of Mental Health.[9] Tumin says for his part, in relation to racial conflict that 'never has social research offered so much substance . . . in such direct relation to particularly urgent problems only to be so rapidly followed by a practice and social policy that takes it exactly in the opposite direction.'[10] That is to say, there can always be, for one reason or another, a gap between operational research and its application.[11] For us, what may be called the 'miscarriages' of operational research cannot be of interest, since we are concerned *a priori* only with the realm of men in the process of acting, and not making imaginary plans for action.

It has similarly been proposed to establish, between pure and applied research, another type, known as directed research.[12] The upholders of this new category, seen as different from the other two, define it thus: (a) pure research occurs within a discipline, and is therefore always specialised. Directed research has as its dimension a whole domain, and thus calls for multi-disciplinarity. (b) It is 'directed' by the resolution of a practical problem which can be, for example, a policy of development. But it leads more to a collection of results than to a solution. Doubtless this collection will—in better encompassing the complexity of phenomena—allow a better solution to be envisaged, one more likely to succeed. But the discovery of this solution is not its goal; the latter will be the task of practitioners who work afterward on the accumulated data. (c) However, in directed research, there is not a separation, but a collaboration of the scholar and the user. Both find themselves linked by the identity of their objective. This means that the results obtained in the course of this collaboration will contribute simultaneously to the advancement of knowledge—accumulation of data obtained on a particular problem—and to the well-being of man—the use of these data for the elaboration of a rational policy. This fusion of scientific and social interests in directed research in effect finds its expression in the programme or project which results from it, a programme or project that consists in an experimental model of change which must then be tested.

Here we near our own perspective. While operational research regards itself as distinct from experimentation, directed research constitutes the first, or the first and second stages of our experimentation. As we know, experimentation is made up of a series of stages: observation of facts; from this observation, elaboration of an explanatory hypothesis taking account of those facts; deduction of the effects following from that hypothesis; new observation, generally in the laboratory, to see if results are produced or not.

Directed research gives us the various data which allow the elaboration both of an hypothesis to explain them and a practice to change them. But there it stops. The manipulation of reality, as the proper realm of research—that is as the last stage of the experimental method—eludes it. In physics, this last stage is the one where the ingenuity of the scholar reveals itself, where his genius appears; how to force the facts to answer a question, by what means can they be made to speak. Why should the same not be true for the social sciences? The upholders of directed research are certainly right in stressing the necessity of applying scientific methods to the processes of change, including voluntary and conscious ones, which unfold in the world. But they remain too much bounded by the division of labour between the 'researcher' and the 'engineer' aiming only to assure their collaboration in the differentiation of tasks.

Applied anthropology on the contrary must follow the experimental method through all its stages—observation, elaboration of an hypothesis (here a practical and not an explanatory one) and the experimental verification of that hypothesis within the field of research, which becomes a laboratory. Once again, it is the science of planned action more than the science of planning thought.

The reader will understand that here we are not criticising either operational or directed research. Besides, the two are so often united that a certain confusion exists between them in the thinking of those who define them. We only wish to distinguish our point of view from those which at first glance might be identified with the one we are advocating. In general, and to sum up our thought, the applied anthropology we are advocating is not the context for collaboration between the researcher and the user; it is the 'pure' or 'basic' science of this context and of 'practice'.

* * *

We believe that we have now sufficiently defined what applied anthropology constitutes for us by means of these various comparisons:

(1) It is a branch of anthropology just as clinical medicine or applied sociology are branches of scientific medicine and general sociology, respectively. In our opinion, it constitutes a new chapter of anthropology, that of *homo moderator rerum*.

(2) It is thus not oriented toward action and planning; it analyses that action and that planning as the old anthropology analysed kinship systems, economic and political institutions, spontaneous

processes of change, and with exactly the same techniques of approach.

But this dual separation—from the old anthropology that studied 'things social' and 'cultures', not their manipulation, and from that which studies social practice in itself—does not prevent applied anthropology from making a basic contribution to general anthropology on the one hand, and to social practice on the other. It would be well to demonstrate this before going farther.

First as to general anthropology. In the first phase, applied anthropology contributes to it in the sense that it allows the revelation of new facts which did not emerge during preceding observation or, if they did emerge, were poorly understood and thus neglected, and taken as of 'little major importance'. American cultural anthropology is currently in the process of making great discoveries in the area of Afro-Americanology. The former type, as with Herskovits, was concerned only with inventorying African survivals among American blacks either in their manifest forms (e.g., Haitian voodoo, Brazilian candomblé) or in their forms 'reinterpreted' in Western terms (e.g., African polygamy reinterpreted in terms of the legitimate wife and the lover; initiative trance reinterpreted in terms of the descent of the Holy Ghost). But the Commission on Public Disorder assembled in the US to formulate programmes for practical action, arrived at the conclusions that two antagonistic societies were developing—in one case the white 'culture' and in the other, a black 'counter-culture' taking exactly the opposite direction from each other.

It is enough to read a book like *The Afro-Americans*[13] to realise all that American cultural anthropology has gained from this 'practical' research which nevertheless was carried out in actional terms: the recognition of non-African 'negro' cultures, whose existence was revealed by British social anthropology and concerning which we have already stressed elsewhere that, at least in certain cases, they take on the aspect of 'counter-cultures'.[14] American cultural anthropology has been so much oriented by its liberalism and optimism that it needed this brutal revelation from applied anthropology for it to be able to head in new directions, more fertile than those taken by the old Afro-Americanist school.

In the second place, general anthropology remained up to our day a science of observation and not an experimental science. And in this it was like almost all the other human sciences, since experimentation on men was condemned in the name of our Western morality. Thus, a whole series of replacements was sought, so that hypotheses could be verified without manipulating persons. Biology, and to a certain extent sociology, used a pathological methodology. Anthropology itself made most use of the comparative method. But, today, policy—and especially that of planned development in underdeveloped countries—constitutes a manipulation of individuals, of their social organisation, in the sense that the planner forces facts to 'speak' in one way or another vis-à-vis the pattern that one wishes to impose on them.

A whole series of causal chains, of at least partial determinisms, may thus be brought to light, which allows us to formulate the laws of the existence or the functioning of societies and cultures, on a less uncertain basis than the mere observation—even of the participant variety—of previous ethnologists.

In introducing new factors, such as money in the exchange process, in causing others to disappear, such as inter-ethnic wars; in changing certain factors as in education, substituting missionary or lay schools for initiation schools, one achieves Stuart Mill's three main types of experimentation—presence, absence and concomitant variation. For example, one sees the introduction of money transform customary marriage practices; the impossibility of inter-tribal warfare is replaced and compensated for by male Don Juanism (and with it the appearance of a new form of eroticism); the change of educational type leads to a subsequent modification of the structure of relations between seniors and juniors.

What is interesting to note here is that these experiments are distinguished—even though they follow Mill's typology—from physics experiments in the sense that they do not have as their goal the verification of hypotheses. Planning acts on social and cultural factors so as to realise practical objectives, not theoretical ones: re the introduction of money, to facilitate exchange, to generalise it, to open it toward the outside; re the disappearance of war, to assure the security of persons and goods and to prevent slavery; re the exchange of tribal initiation for schools, to enlarge the information field and thus to permit the technical progress of the country. The results which occur are not foreseen, or desired by the manipulators.

The gap between the fixed 'objective' and the sociological 'effect' of change means that anthropological experimentation has more the character of what Bernard calls an 'experiment to see'. That is to say, it is in order to discover new laws rather than to verify their presumed existence. It is still true that policy allows cultural and social anthropology to progress from the descriptive or typological to the explanatory, to discover correlations, to recognise chains of determinations, independent of the will of men. That is, it brings us to the recognition of scientific laws that we could only with difficulty have arrived at by the comparative method alone. Operational or directed research, in face of failure, consoles itself by saying that the latter is due to resistance to change. But applied anthropology allows general anthropology to distinguish several types of resistance, those which derive from the will of men whom one wishes to force to change their habits, and those which derive from the existence of social and cultural laws. It allows it to outline the fields of determinisms.

It also permits the outlining of their limits. And this is why, if on the one hand it makes a valuable contribution to the elaboration of a more fully scientific general anthropology, it also makes an important contribution to the practical application of anthropology to social development and to cultural mutation. If, in fact, changes do not occur just anyhow, but follow a certain number of rules that applied anthropology can discover, and if they obey a certain number of laws, then determining factors can be more readily controlled, change more surely directed, the unexpected results of formerly purely rational planning can be foreseen, and effective measures thus put into effect to eliminate their negative aspects.

Of course, account must always be taken of the gestalt aspect of each culture, of the fact that each culture item, and the function it fulfills is specific to the global context—which means that the change of one such item, whose positive effects have been assured for a given culture, may not have the same results if introduced into another gestalt. Obviously, account must also be taken of the classic distinction between overt and covert culture. Many programmes have failed because they were made to function only in terms of overt culture. This is why, in respecting the laws and determinism of manifest culture, proposed innovations that find themselves in conflict with covert meanings characteristic of a given culture are bound to fail. But always, in both sorts of case, there is no effective practice without a respect for determinism; that is, without a preliminary transformation of rational into experimental research.

Yet there is another contribution of applied anthropology to social practice, which, though less obvious (or at least less often shown until recently, and let us say as regards France, until May 1968) is not less significant, namely its influence on the value system. We have said much in the preceding chapter about ideologies which underlie research. We have been able to do this because applied anthropology, in the sense in which it is usually understood, has most often resulted in failure, struggling against resistance. It has now been more clearly realised than before that anthropologists carry with them ends, values and norms borrowed from their ethnic or national backgrounds and that, consequently, the models of change and proposed innovations are a mixture of value judgements and reality judgements.

But we can go further, to 'scientific truth'. In so far as science has become more an elaboration of models and a sort of operational machine, a new ideology has appeared—no longer ethnic but that of a particular class, constituted by the international community of specialists. It is not without caution that we have been able to speak of the underdevelopment of sociology, or even its demise. Rationalism, with its values, ends and norms, can also be considered as a 'distortion' of reality. As long as sociology was content to remain a descriptive and explanatory science, this element of distortion did not appear clearly: Marx respected the laws of science; Mannheim distinguished scientific from political knowledge. But once sociology became an applied sociology, then the role of ideology which had remained hidden, became suddenly clarified, by means of the manipulation it claimed to exert on reality.

And what may be said of applied sociology is also true of anthropology. Thus we see more and more the criticism by youth, not of governmental directives and activities in planning and development (this has always taken place, and if it is possible to say that the May revolution was a failure, it is because it found itself blocked at the level of political criticism) but of the claim of science and of reason to 'lord it over' the world, which is going much too far. For the scholar is no longer attacked as a 'watchdog' of his society, and subject to its policies, but *qua* scholar.

However, at the same time that applied anthropology leads to a critique of rational activity, and of the practice which it entails, it also, paradoxically, allows us to elucidate new systems of ends, values and norms for man. This same youth that fought against 'academic' science and establishment traditions, rediscovered Comte, Proudhon and Fourier.

What characterised that 'humanist' sociology at the beginning of the nineteenth century as opposed to the 'scientific' sociology of the twentieth is that it tried to disentangle from observation of the facts (law of the three states, distinction of organic periods and periods of crisis—creative value of conflict—universal attraction) new goals allied to new visions of the world. It is that it contributed both to giving sense to life and to changing the established order. Radical student movements tend to place themselves outside the development of social sciences modelled on the natural sciences, to discover values and goals issuing less from rational thought than from creative action. We believe that this mutation of affectivity and intelligence in the younger generation is the fruit—no doubt unexpected—of the development of applied or 'Promethean' sciences. But (and this is what we register ourselves as against) it is a reaction against the crucifixion of Prometheus on the Caucasus, and against the circling vulture; that is to say, against the punishment of *hubris*.

In any case, applied anthropology—even if it is pure science—makes a double contribution to what may be designated as an art of action, in causing it to take critical cognisance of its ends and in analysing the differential reasons for achieved action and for failure.

*   *   *

R. N. Adams distinguishes two types of applied anthropology[15] corresponding broadly to preventive medicine and curative medicine. The former has its place at the beginning of action, before the introduction of innovations into a local regional or national community. It includes the ethnographic analysis of that community, to try to foresee what will result from the introduction of these innovations and also to devise the best strategy of action—reformative or revolutionary.

The second has its place after action, for the ends realised often bring unintended side-effects, and negative results—destruction of family bonds, development of mental illness or of juvenile delinquency, greater inequality between men after than before the intervention. It is thus necessary to examine the new situation that has been established to try to reconstruct it in proposing concrete measures destined to remedy those pathological phenomena that have involuntarily been brought about.

Thus the schema of applied anthropology has reversed itself in its stages, from the nineteenth to the twentieth century. While the rhythm of change was slow, the corrective came before the preventive. When troubles appeared—troubles which were generally local either in certain sectors of a population, or of the global culture—applied anthropology only responded by finding adequate remedies for them. But today, with the acceleration of rhythms of social and cultural change, one cannot wait for phenomena to manifest themselves before acting; action must be taken before events. The role of prevention surpasses that of therapy. And if therapy is necessary, it only comes later.

This change of perspective, from action in the present to action projected for the future, naturally led anthropologists to devise models of intervention obeying the methodological rules of science. It is these models we spoke of above, under the name of operational and directed research. Applied anthropology, as we have defined it, does not apply value judgements to its models; it considers them as social *institutions* at the same level as the family, economics, or politics. True, they are institutions of innovative action, but still institutions of the same nature as the others, which themselves are institutions of crystallised action. They can thus be the object of similar analyses.

In brief, we propose to consider 'projected actions' as 'cultural works' of the same order as all the other works of man, e.g., his kinship system, his organisation into castes or classes. As for the other cultural works, we can discern here laws of functioning, chains of links between the parts. . . . However, there is still a difference; the norms of operational and directed research control the behaviour of planners just as the cultural norms transmitted through enculturation control the conduct of social actors; but from the outset they are not of the same order. The latter are constituted by ultimately unconscious determinants; the former are always conscious (the only unconscious elements to be found among them are values that have remained latent and have been translated into objectives). Briefly, on the one hand there are rules, and on the other, laws.[16]

At a second stage our applied anthropology will have to examine the problem of the relation between the rules of reason that have presided over the elaboration of these projects or of these operational models, and the laws of social nature. There we have, if you like, the old philosophical problem: are the laws of the mind the same as those of things? But this problem will not be treated philosophically, even if it tends toward philosophy. It will be posed by a scientific analysis, no longer this time of the institution as a cultural work, created by man's reason, but as an institution functioning in the concrete reality of the society of men. We may take some examples:

In a project to lay out underdeveloped territories, it will study the dialectical relations that can be established between artificially structured space and the natural structure of extra space (precisely of two spaces, ecological and cultural). Or again, in a policy of industrialisation of an agricultural country, the dialectical relations between the mathematical time of the clock and the duration lived to the rhythm of the soil or vegetation. Planners designate this confrontation between the results of their intervention and the objectives of their projects by the term 'evaluation'. But in ordinary applied anthropology, this evaluation is thought of in terms of action—success or failure—while in applied anthropology as we conceive it, it should be thought of in terms of thresholds of intervention, of their elasticity, of limits, of finitude; that is, in conceptual terms.

Let us return to the experimental method with which we identified our applied anthropology. The technique of the scholar is—like that of the planner—an active method of production, of direction of events; in both cases, there is an alteration of the real, a modification of given situations.[17] But must we conclude from this that the old dogma of the rigidity of the laws of nature should be abandoned?

In part, yes, but only in part. For nature responds in a certain way to the question that is posed to it, and if the scholar does force things to speak to him, he listens afterward to their words. This is true even though in another realm, that of social and not physical experimentation—that is in a realm where the law of recurrence is in play—there is also a 'response' from social nature to the question asked by fabricating reason. And it is on the existence of these 'responses' that we relied above to show the relevance of applied anthropology for the constitution of a truly scientific general theoretical anthropology.

The operational model of intervention or innovation is a system of thought directed toward action. But this system is manipulated by men concentrating first on the elaboration of the best possible model, then on the transformation of directive ideas into social forces of change. Applied anthropology owes it to itself to study these projects and plans as groupings of individuals in inter-action. For it is only through the human psyche and the group that the metamorphosis of ideas into social forces can take place. This study poses a certain number of problems which can become the object of scientific inquiry and certain of which have already given rise to promising research.

An example is the problem of communication and the distor-tion that the receiver causes the message to undergo. It is thus that, for many administrators, governors and even more for the masses, emitted ideas of planning, industrialisation, or socialism are immediately transformed into 'myths' instead of remaining a set of 'programmes'; which is one way to prevent the metamorphosis of the idea into an acting force within reality; the force is diverted into an expression of the imaginary. Or again, there is the inverse phenomenon where negative evaluations develop a complex which a Tunisian sociologist, Boudheba, has called the 'complex of underdevelopment' and which risks aborting experiments by overestimating the difficulties encountered in the first survey of the procedure which has been undertaken. In this latter case, it is no longer the innovative idea that becomes operative, it is the 'obstacles', on the contrary, that become more powerful counter-forces.

We also have data already on the relations between researchers in multi-disciplinary research, or in Institutes, public or private, charged with formulating development programmes. We also have data on team work of social engineers or expert anthropolo-gists—especially regarding human relations, discussion, conflict, and participation between programmers and users. A very fine book by Duvignaud[18] shows us how an experiment—one which is moreover as much an experiment of theoretical or empirical anthropology as of applied anthropology—led to a change both in the anthropologists and in the natives. The natives are no longer the same as they were before the arrival of the ethnologists; they have opened themselves up to certain outside influences. The anthropologists have learned uneasiness; they have realised that things are not so simple as they had imagined; they have passed from an abstract notion of man to a knowledge of real men.

However, all the studies we have at our disposal are still fragmentary. We know that man transforms himself in transforming things, but we do not know how or why. We know that things only allow themselves to be manipulated within certain limits, and that men who manipulate them are themselves manipulated. But we do not know the underlying determinants of this dual manipulation.

The anthropologist should, no doubt, continue to describe existing societies and cultures for the world. And today there are no more primitives, there are only societies 'in transition' and cultures become syncretistic (since they mix, sometimes in conflicting wholes, 'modern' with 'archaic' values). But to discover the laws of social 'transition' as well as the mechanisms of cultural syncretism, it is necessary to build an anthropology of *homo aleator et moderator rerum* from which one could no doubt later draw an applied art, but which should remain for the moment a purely theoretical science and not, as it has been till today, a practice calling itself scientific.

NOTES

1. A. H. Leighton, 'Applied Research and Pure Research', *Amer. Anthrop.*, 48, 1946.
2. G. G. Granger, *Méthodologie Économique*, Presses Universitaires de France, Paris, 1955.
3. Max Pagès, *La vie affective des groupes*, Dunod, Paris, 1968.
4. F. Fernandes, *Ensaios de Sociologia General e Aplicada*, S. Paulo, 1960.
5. H. Freyer, *La Sociologie, science de la réalité*, from the Spanish translation, Mexico, 1944.
6. K. Mannheim, *Freedom, Power and Democratic Planning*, Int. Lib. of Sociology and Social Reconstruction, New York, 1950.

7. One distinguishes the 'objective' from the 'mission' or, if one prefers, from the end that the user has fixed by its quantifiable character. The end gives a direction to the objectives. The objectives translate the end, which, without that would remain a simple aspiration, into precise and measurable finalities. For example, the end: to struggle for the amelioration of physical or mental health, translates itself into the following objectives: how many doctors to train, hospitals to build, and beds to plan for, etc.

8. A. B. Cherns, 'Les rapports entre les institutions de recherche et les utilisateurs de la recherche', R.I.S.S., UNESCO, XXII, 2, 1970.

9. H. Orlans, *The Use of Social Research in Federal Domestic Programs*, Washington, 4 vols., 1967.

10. M. Tumin, 'Some Social Consequences of Research on Racial Relations', *Amer. Sociologist*, 3, 2, 1968.

11. Our quotation is taken from B-P Lecuyer, 'L'apport des sciences sociales à l'orientation de l'activité nationale', R.I.S.S., UNESCO, XXII, 2, 1970, p. 320.

12. E. Trist, 'Les institutions de recherche sociale', R.I.S.S., op. cit., pp. 334–8.

13. Szwed and Whitten (eds.), *Afro-American Anthropology: Contemporary Perspectives*, New York, 1969.

14. R. Bastide, *Les Amériques Noires*, Payot, Paris, 1967.

15. R. N. Adams, op. cit.

16. Perhaps there might be some interest in rereading here the founder of technology, Espinas: 'Science is a world of representation, act is a world of action . . . One is a set of types of laws, expression of the necessary relations of simultaneous movements observed in nature up to now; the other is a set of models and rules, enjoining men to act in a certain manner in the future . . . Also, despite some abstractions that practical theory may raise, it can never forget that it is called upon to realise itself in concrete, given conditions . . . Art is submitted before all things to the consideration of the possible. That which is not possible, given present or future reality, is not in its domain: to wish for the

impossible is contradictory. One should thus consider arts as practical . . . They are the conditions of existence for human societies, as instincts are the conditions of existence of animal societies. They are the responses motivating responses corresponding to the image that societies make of the world and of themselves, and destined to provide in their combination for the conservation and progress of the group.'

17. Cf. the ideas of John Dewey in *Experience and Nature*, Chicago and London, 1925, for example, which is at the origin of the American effort to reconcile knowledge and action, in making of knowledge 'a case of directed activity instead of being something independent of action'. While for his part he considered action as intelligence realising itself in nature: 'Man's intelligent activity is not something that it introduced into nature from without; it is nature realising its own potentialities in view of a fuller and richer production of events.' (*The Quest for Certainty*, George Allen & Unwin, London, 1930.)

18. J. Duvignaud, *Chebika*, Gallimard, Paris, 1968.

Anthropology Applied to Race Relations

13

To make our conception of applied anthropology more explicit in relation to the one which is currently accepted, we shall take another example. We may be excused if we choose it not from the realm of development—since the author has never studied that personally—even though it is linked to it, as we shall see, but instead from that of race relations. For the latter has always been important to us, and the author has carefully followed all the proposed solutions, as well as participating in certain programmes charged with providing a solution to inter-racial conflicts.

The first point that emerges from an examination of the programmes recommended is that they are linked to the postulates, characteristics and methods of science. Still, science changes over time and, with it, the proposals of practical projects. That is, apart from ideologies or ethical finalities, there is an orientation of practice in terms of the orientation of the conception which the community of scholars has, at a given time, of what authentic science may be.

For example, the racial problem was first attacked in the United States at the time of curative rather than of preventive applied anthropology, linked to 'social problems' rather than to the planning of reality, through an anthropology based on the factorial analysis of social situations. Thus, à propos the Chicago riots, the experts successively passed in review all the factors that could have provoked them—analysis of racial stereotypes, of opinions, of the economic, political, social, professional and union relations between whites and blacks—so as to discover among them the causes of tensions. However, these tensions had long remained latent; why did they explode at a given point? The reasons suggested by people who were interviewed were only rationalisations that hid actual factors. It was the active but hidden forces that had to be found underneath—exodus of negroes from the south to the north, growth of the black ghetto, economic depression.

From this sort of research, which schematises a situation, an equally fragmented 'application' will emerge; an appropriate solution will be proposed for each causal factor, e.g., a change in the content of education to change mentalities, building of better apartments for the descendants of Africans, and even mixed residences to respond to the growth of the black ghetto. Recommendations will be made to the urban masses of unskilled workers through the intermediary of union leaders so that blacks will not become strike breakers, etc.

With Myrdal, we proceed from the application of an analytic model to that of an economic one. That is to say, Myrdal thought it was possible to apply to the racial problem the same method used by the economist to establish a price index or a standard of living. Each index is an average of all the different variables combined in the phenomenon concerned, which means that if one of these variables is changed, all the others will be affected. This is the theory of cumulative causation. An improvement in one of the elements of a situation will have throughout—allowance made for the psycho-sociological resistances it will arouse—an effect on all the other elements, finally modifying the entire situation. It matters little which one is attacked. Thus, favourable modifications in employment conditions, and housing of blacks may be translated into a diminution of the discrimination of prejudiced whites, just as attenuation of white prejudice may lead to an improvement of the professional, social and cultural status of blacks. In any case, it is never possible altogether to eliminate racial misunderstanding by using one lever; it is necessary to act on several points at once and to find the most strategic ones.

Myrdal believed that these strategic points are provided by the democratic ideal fostered by the American whites. This ideal is manifested in laws. A certain number of institutions, e.g., the state, the courts and the unions cannot depart too far from the law. So these are the institutions that present the strategic points for selective action; from there on, to the extent that, in the framework of these institutions, contacts occur most frequently, segments of prejudice will crumble one after another. And this is the 'snowball effect', which grows as it rolls.

In the second place, since on the one hand there are proposed applications resulting from theoretical research, and on the other, the builders of theories who are in disaccord since they are engaged in different disciplines, we must observe that the realm of action is dependent on the state of the 'republic of intellectuals' at a given time, and its division into 'classes'. There is, for example, a psycho-social notion that links group behaviour to the individual behaviour that composes it, for, they point out, racial conflicts are not rational. Reason cannot abolish them, and because this is so, they must derive from another source. They are the expression of unconscious complexes of an affective kind (the transfer of aggression for example on to a scapegoat) or of a particular personality type, e.g., Adorno's authoritarian personality.

Sociologists, on the contrary, do not accept at all the idea that the social derives from the individual; one must begin with the distinction between in-group and out-group and as a result, they say, it is less the individual who needs reforming—by education or psycho-therapy—than social institutions. The accent is placed on politics. Doubtless, one can state that laws will not be accepted—except when they are just—that legislation cannot fight prejudice, but only control behaviour. However, by establishing social conditions of equality of statuses, legislation leads indirectly to diminish prejudice. Above all, legislative measures bring to light more brutally the existence of marginal minority groups and give them confidence to undertake the struggle against privileged groups. In brief, they can both develop feelings of security in blacks and stimulate them to fight to overcome their inequality with whites.

Marxists believe that racism is merely a rationalisation by the dominant classes to justify an exploitation of the capitalist variety. There will thus be no other effective remedy than that of changing the economic structure. Closer to our own position, a 'semantic' tendency develops that affirms that conflicts are not due to an incompatibility of values or of goals, but result from mutual verbal or conceptual incomprehensions. If we can understand each other, that is, communicate, then conflicts will diminish or disappear.[1] But what concerns us in applied anthropology is less the scientific analysis of theoretical postulates, even though this is an important aspect, than the scientific analysis of the 'application' drawn from them, that is of action in the process of occurring.

We have defined actions as experiments. The main variables that have been experimented on are: educational methods, programmes of contact between individuals of different races, projects of training Lewinian groups, propagandist action. . . . These experiments have encountered great difficulties. Attitudes must be measured before and after the experience; these measurements are done by verbal responses to questionnaires; how can one be sure that these verbal responses correspond to actual behaviour? One must isolate the action of the variable in question from that of others that act at the same time, e.g., to isolate the action of teachers on the child from other factors that influence him, such as the comics he reads, the radio he listens to, the action of his playmates, and that of his parents. Finally, a control group must be formed.

Thus, in the case we have been discussing, another group of students must be found with a population of the same ages and IQs, whose parents have the same social status, and who have answered the first questionnaire by expressing the same prejudices; that is, one identical in all respects to the experimental group except that it does not receive the same 'race education'. Even if one succeeds approximatively, since the experience is a long one of several weeks, it is impossible to prevent the children of the two groups from communicating with each other, which means that the control group is contaminated by the experimental group. It is therefore very difficult to judge the success or failure of such experiments.

Nevertheless, a certain number of measures for the evaluation of the results of an action have been proposed, e.g., through the 'social barometer', the number of complaints received by the police; incidents in bars, in restaurants, in employment agencies, etc. (the temperature of conflict either rises or falls). Further, interviewing of a representative population in a community that one wishes to change before and after a programme against discrimination has been suggested, e.g. in a church by means of indices of participation before and after the joining of blacks and whites in common activities.

Social anthropology has at its disposal a large number of such experiments—in the army (Stauffer, *The American Soldier*, I, Ch. 10); in mixed housing (Deutsch-Collins, 1949); in play groups (Axlène, 'Play Therapy and Race Conflict')[2]; in the content of education (Cook, 1950); in the structure of the school system (Brameld, 1946); in the formation of institutionalised relations between whites and blacks (Smith, 'An Experiment in Modifying Attitudes Toward the Negro'); on the role of films in the fight against racism (Cooper and Dinerman, 1951), just to mention some examples of research carried out between 1945 and 1950. We will not stop here to discuss the contradictory results of these experiments, but they provide applied anthropology with an excellent source of data for the description of actional strategies that seek to modify reality.

These are of course micro-actions, and the procedures they put into effect cannot be generalised to macro-actions. All the same, they bring to light a certain number of interesting facts. Thus, it appears that inter-racial propaganda is only accepted by individuals who are already against racism; others distort the message and find in it new reasons to persist in their prejudices; that everything depends on the context in which the propaganda is spread (the same public that, in 1951, enthusiastically applauded the film 'The Sound of Fury', concerned with the resolution of racial problems, shortly thereafter booed a speech by Senator Taft which defended ideas similar to those applauded in the film); that everything depends on the social classes addressed. Ordinary people respond better to sentimental appeals which on the other hand, repel intellectuals. In any case, the current is soon reversed, and they return quickly to their old prejudice with an even greater intensity in that their sensibilities were affected for a moment by means of a propaganda which now seems repugnant to them.

Up to now, we have only been alluding to the research and practice of psychologists and sociologists, since we have taken all our examples from the United States and in the period before 1960, that is, a period when this problem was neglected by anthropologists and considered as the concern of applied sociology and psychology. But this does not mean that these 'actions' by sociologists to change situations, and those of psychologists to transform attitudes, have no interest for applied anthropology as we have defined it—as the study of man acting on reality in order to change it. It matters little to us if the modificatory action is that of a sociologist or a psychologist and not of a professional anthropologist, since in all these cases it is so-called 'rational' actions that are at issue.

We must consider the whole set of attempts made, projects elaborated, and operational research as constituting a documentation of the first rank for the discovery of (1) the laws of considered or scientific action and (2) the obstacles encountered; and from their analysis, to come back to (1) the evaluation of the place or function of postulates, scientific methods and techniques in directed action and (2) the study of interpersonal relations within the context of paternalist, authoritarian or democratic action; (3) the examination of the influence of underlying myths (belief in progress, in the value of reason, optimism concerning the action of science, liberalism). This will enable us to formulate a dialectic of reason and facts, logical rules and the laws of social nature, with all the phenomena we have enumerated throughout the preceding chapters—those of recurrence, of intervention thresholds, of the play of unconscious factors in the very process of conscious and voluntary action.

But clearly, in a book on applied anthropology, we must emphasise more especially the experiences of anthropologists. Basically, what is postulated by sociological or psychological experimentation is the identity of reason among all men, regardless of the colour of their skin. Culture is denied as a moulding force of specific forms of reasoning, of ways of thinking and feeling. In vain has Herskovits tried to show that the North American negro had, like the Latin American negro, an 'African heritage'. The sociologist or psychologist saw the blacks of the US as differing from whites only in terms of physical characteristics. And if occasionally they spoke of acculturation, for them it meant the passage from a zero-point of culture (slavery having destroyed the African civilisations and replaced them with nothing) to the culture of the lower middle class.

The majority of anthropologists sharing this point of view abandoned the study of the ghettos and their possible transformation to sociologists and psychologists, to concern themselves only with the Indians. It was a rude awakening: the increase of black riots, the desire for 'black power', the unexpected response of the coloured masses to a white policy of liberalisation in terms of a refusal to cooperate, and segregation in relation to the activity of 'white liberals', so as to re-erect the barriers wherever the whites broke them down, posed new problems to specialists in race relations. What was wrong with the transformation projects that had been elaborated to resolve the race problem? Was it the parcelling out of so-called 'abnormal' situations into dependent and independent variables? Was it the surreptitious introduction of white values into the proposed solutions? In the latter case, the failure also came from the existence of African or neo-African values. To the cultural stimuli of whites, the Negroes responded with reactions that were culturally non-white.

Thus, American cultural anthropology came in its turn to be interested in the race problem. In fact, even aside from Herskovits, Dollard and Powdermaker had been interested in it when the blacks were massed in the south. But if the existence of negro culture had been affirmed—with its eroticism, affective religiosity, and irrationalism—it was defined as a culture of the lower class or, if you will, as a 'folk culture'. With the black exodus from the fields of the south to the metropolitan areas of the north, they postulated that urbanisation would destroy this folk culture. And it was from that point on that anthropology delegated its powers of describing reality and its possible manipulations to the sociologists as specialists in urban problems.

It seems to us that the return of cultural anthropology, following the failure of sociology, was made in two stages. First, there was the discovery of a new type of culture, which had not been perceived by the old anthropology but which was to be brought to light by rapid economic and social development, widening the economic gap between those who profited by it and those who were its victims, and thereby yielding 'the culture of poverty' or rather, the 'culture of misery'. One clearly sees this is a transitional solution. For if one recognises the existence of the culture of the negro ghettos, that culture is of the same kind as that of Indians or poor whites in analogous situations, since it is determined by the conditions of economic life. And the laws of 'deprivation' can only be of the same nature regardless of the ethnic stock with which one is dealing.

In the second stage, a new concept was discovered—that of 'counter-culture'. Here one makes the observation that a specific negro culture exists. The blacks—the better to show their non-identification with the whites and their middle class values—adopt the opposite of white middle class behaviour—the extolling of male virility as against what has been called the American matriarchy, of sexuality and violence as against Protestant puritanism, the creation of a language unintelligible to non-blacks, of musical and gestural expressions in reaction to Westernised jazz and ballroom dancing. Obviously, one can conceive of the existence of a culture reacting to the discriminatory policy of the whites, which will be simply a 'counter-culture'. It will then be only a pseudo-culture since it is a culture of defense, a protective skill, not life.

Our applied anthropology in any case owes it to itself to integrate this counter-culture into its research, for it constitutes one of the laws of human action: all manipulative action tends to provoke defensive reactions in the manipulated group. What is called 'resistance to change' then no longer seems to consist of the weight of former traditions and habits, but rather of a will to discover its identity and desires, and to specify itself as 'other'.

But from the beginning of the analysis of this counter-culture, anthropologists have had to verify the existence of a negro culture—non-African and in the process of formation—a culture, then, not yet completed (but then what culture is ever completed?) that could be called a 'prospective' culture since it is oriented toward creating a positive 'negritude'. The black creates for himself, for example, his own history, which is no longer a section of North American history but his 'own' history of the black people; he re-integrates himself into the past; he gives himself a collective memory. Or again, over and above the old folklore of his folk culture, he gives himself new cultural expressions which can certainly withstand the influence of certain sections of whites equally in revolt against American society, especially the hippies, but which are nonetheless the discoveries of negritude.

A certain number of facts—the extension of relations between Afro-Americans and Afro-Africans, the arrival of what might be called 'missionaries' of 'fetishist' religions in Harlem, and still others—seem to presage that this negro culture will root itself more and more deeply in the humus of American soil. And this all the more easily because—here Herskovits is vindicated— African civilisations were able to continue subterraneously in tendential forms in the negro population of the United States right under the near-sighted eyes of sociologists and psychologists. For the moment, the new American cultural anthropology remains there, with the description of reality, the empirical enumeration of facts, and the search for new concepts. It has not, to our knowledge, elaborated a new strategy to modify this state of affairs in the old applied anthropological sense.

We take the view that if we wish to discover the laws of men's manipulative action, the casual laws that in these manipulations lead to effects of controlled variation of the acting factors, we must go beyond monography to engage ourselves in comparative anthropology. For all multi-racial societies pose problems, and everywhere there are responses to action, manipulations, programming, or planning on the part of governments and the scholars who advise them. Here we shall take two examples from two extremes of a bi-polar continuum, that of South Africa and that of a 'racial democracy' (to be clearly distinguished from a political or economic democracy), that of Brazil.

In South Africa, white policy took the opposite direction from the liberal North American one. White American liberals wished to fight against segregation, the caste system, and to integrate the blacks into the global society. The politicians of South Africa want to separate the Africans of colour from the white society culturally. They wish, via reservations or 'independent states', to 'retribalise' the Africans. We will not go into the contradictions of the system deriving from the fact that white industry has need of the unskilled labour of the people of colour, and thus that retribalisation conflicts with the necessity for a certain acculturation. (To which should be added that the whites must take account of the pressure from international society in favour of the development of underdeveloped peoples, whence comes their proposition of dual development of whites and blacks, each according to the values of their own culture.)

In any case, and speaking broadly, South Africa proposes 'negritude' to its natives. And from this stems a different reaction from the one we have just summarised for the United States. While in the latter country, to a liberal integrationist assimilative policy, the negro responds with negritude, in South Africa, to a segregationist tribalising policy of cultural separation, the black responds with the repudiation of negritude, and a desire for integration, assimilation and Westernisation. These reactions are then opposite, but the law that explains them remains the same: to take the opposite position to that of manipulators and planners because manipulations and plans are firstly the work of outsiders, and secondly, even if they seek the participation of the various groups concerned, they are always made for the profit of the politically dominant group.

In Brazil, the situation is different. Not that there is not generally a colour-prejudice (against the negro, but not against the mulatto) and even sometimes race-prejudice (more against the mulatto than the negro) but the prejudices are always individual and not collective, and therefore not institutionalised. Race relations—except in the industrialised areas, where there is a more bitter competition in the employment market—are regulated by a paternalistic-type structure, that allows the integration of the black into the global society, but in the lower strata of the population. Prejudice has no raison d'être in a paternalistic society since the function of prejudice is to react against the rise of the black, and since the policy it brings into play—through discrimination in employment, housing, education, unions and elections—is to 'put the negro in his place'. Paternalism has the same result, without tensions: the negro, castrated in his aggression by the affective relations he may have with his white master, who is his protector, 'stays in his place' by himself—at the very bottom of the social ladder. Or, when he resists, his upward mobility remains under the control of the white, and as a result he will always owe something to the white who has given him respect and recognition.

If we leave aside the industrial regions, like Sao Paulo, where the blacks are also becoming integrated, but to the class society, and where competition between races will take place not in the proletariat—which is a recent phenomenon—what will be the reaction of the black to the paternalistic type of manipulation? First, because generally the mulatto is less debarred than the black, there is the desire for miscegenation which the negroes call 'purging the blood' by causing the progressive disappearance of the black stain that blots them. Secondly, there is the desire to internalise white values, to become what the whites call 'negroes with white souls'. What roles can negritude play in such a situation in Brazil?

If the black must internalise white values, he must equally internalise the image that whites have of blacks. Whites think that blacks have an innate sense of rhythm, of musical improvisation, that their syncretic Afro-Brazilian folklore has great value for international propaganda, at a time when the West is interested in negro music and dance. As a result, the black will model himself on this image and respond to this white society in the way he is expected to. He will be—on the radio, on TV, and in the ever more commercialised carnivals—the carrier of the culture expected by the whites. We see therefore that these responses of blacks to their manipulators depend not only on the stimuli imposed on them by the white world, but also on the socio-cultural context within which causal chains are established.

Nonetheless, the paternalistic model of race relations is disappearing with rapid economic and social development in the states of Latin America. And it is on the basis of this state of transition, between the old and the new America, that classical applied anthropology was led to propose plans for intervention. In effect, development, far from making inequalities disappear, widens the gap separating the various social strata. In the first stage, anthropologists verified the existence of a duality between progressive and traditional sectors. They therefore elaborated their plans with a view to the disappearance of this duality, to make traditional sectors pass into the progressive sector. But they perceived that the traditional sector did not subsist as a 'resistance' to development, as a refractory sector, because its population retains a preindustrial mentality which is difficult to change. Rather, it subsisted because the 'underdevelopment' of one part of the country was an integral part of the 'development' of the other. The traditional sector is not traditional because it rejects change. It is rather an artefact of change itself, which leads inevitably to the greater marginalisation of the rural masses in the countryside, as unskilled manpower to be conserved for the future, more or less as permanently unemployed or under-employed in the bidonvilles of national and regional capitals, and as an unskilled mass to keep wages from rising, which makes industry non-competitive.

Development policies should then be complemented by a policy of fighting against certain of its negative effects, and anthropologists will then be called upon to elaborate tactics of de-marginalisation, e.g., plans of agrarian reform and transformations of bidonvilles into working-class quarters.

We said at the beginning of this chapter that the problem of race relations would at a given point lead to the problem of economic and social development. This is the fashion in applied anthropology today—and not only for the Caribbean or for South America, but also for the negroes of the United States—to the extent that North American anthropologists think that the culture of these blacks is only a culture of poverty, and that it will thus suffice to raise their standard of living for tension between the two races to disappear.

This is possible. But we will only be sure of it when the various reactions of Indians, negroes, half-castes and poor whites to these development policies have been studied. Since, by definition, these policies consider individuals not in terms of their racial or ethnic origins, but only as 'marginal', or sharing a 'common state of poverty' they have neglected the cultural variable so as to hold fast to the economic one. The stimulation of development constitutes an experiment in the context of our applied anthropology; it must be closely followed up and we have always asked our students who are interested in it not to forget to evaluate its results according to the various racial sections of the population. In effect, certain observations have already been made, but in a more impressionistic than truly scientific way, showing that:

(1) In Guatemala, blacks are considered as *ladinos*, that is as 'Westerners' as opposed to Indians.

(2) In the impoverished villages of Peru, the Indian reacts to his situation more by passivity and schizoid behaviour, while the black reacts more by aggression and more spirited behaviour. But is this as a black, or is it as a member of a minority group in the bidonvilles?

(3) The survey conducted by Fernandes and the author in the slums of Sao Paulo revealed to us the existence of a phenomenon of imitation of foreigners who had emigrated to Brazil by blacks who understood through them the mechanisms of vertical mobility, and who were thus led to distinguish between 'possible profession' (mechanic, electrician, taxi-driver) and the 'desired profession' for which they had hoped before, as a reaction to the system of slavery and in association with the 'complex of the white hand' that this system had developed in Latin America (liberal professions were lower-paid in the tertiary sector than in the secondary sector).

But these few observations naturally cannot permit any generalisations, since they belong to very different social or cultural contexts.

We can stop here. For our survey of dissenting youth and political radicals, when we asked them about the problem of multi-racial societies, showed us that they saw no other solution than economic and social development of the dominated or exploited classes, in terms of a socialist system of values. It is not with impunity that in this perspective they consider negritude as their bête noire, whether they see in it a racist or even fascist reaction, or whether they see in it the greatest obstacle to be conquered to achieve the realisation of their aims (negritude being in their opinion linked to the existence of a mystical and pre-industrial mentality, and forming for them, e.g., in Haiti, the modern form of what religion had been for the European proletariat—an 'opium' to make the people 'sleep' more deeply).

We believe that applied anthropology as a theoretical science must analyse this operational model, as it has analysed others, in its hidden motivations as well as in its plans for social reality. And to the extent that it proceeds from thought action to real action—e.g., in the form of urban guerilla movements—to analyse the dialectic of actions and reactions, the limits of participation of the various races in a common task, the cultural variables that will be shaken up in this agitation, both as causes (stimuli and curbs) and as effects—the eventual birth of a new culture or a greater homo-genisation within our ethnocentric and Western vision of men and of the world.

NOTES

1. Cf. J. Bernard, *Current Research in the Sociology of Conflict*, Congrès de Liège de l'Association Internationale de Sociologie, 1953; G. W. Allport, *The Resolution of Inter-Group Tensions*, Geneva, 1952.
2. A. Axlène, 'Play Therapy and Race Conflict', *Journ. of Abnormal and Social Psych.*, 43, 1948.

By Way of Conclusion: 14
Rationality and the Irrational

In a preceding chapter, we cited a text by Meillassoux concerning the sumptuary economy in which he protests against the qualification 'irrational' given it by economists, and shows that it is simply another rationality that is at issue. We ourselves have insisted on the diversity of forms of reasoning—by correspondences or categorisation, by symbols or by signs—and we have declared that we must not emasculate reason by considering as valuable only one of its aspects at the expense of the richness of its operational mechanisms.

Cournot proposed a law of three states that showed humanity as evolving from biological determinism (of 'real primitives', i.e. vitalism) to the pure determinism of all our behaviour by reason (rationalism) passing by way of an intermediate historical phase where action remains unpredictable because subject to the hazards of chance and of freedom. Thus, housing responds to an original instinct for security, but from this the town develops at the will of historical events, being restricted or enlarged, grouping its houses along winding streets near the church, or in improvised quarters around the factory. But already, with urbanism, reason dictates its geometric maps to the builders of the future.

The existence of an applied anthropology seems to support Cournot. But have we really emerged from history? For the following problem arises in terms of this book, which has defended the experimental point of view as against the rational: to know whether the conception of reason is not itself a product of history, that is, the result of multiple entangled causes of a social nature, and consequently, their uncertain result since it is conjectural and not structural.

We pose this problem because the action of planners encounters obstacles and resistances as we have seen throughout. An applied anthropology as we have defined it—as an experimental science— is not surprised by obstacles or resistances, for it sees them as a response of facts to the hypotheses of those who wish to manipulate them. It allows the discovery of laws of society or of culture, laws which—once known—make possible an 'art' but no longer a science of human action on things.

On the other hand, from the perspective of classical applied anthropology, these obstacles and resistances seem non-rational— suspicions rooted in mentalities, desires not to change pleasant habits, for the privileged, fear of losing their status—the anxiety of men faced with the adventure of change. A background of Manichaeanism is thus delimited in the minds of planners, who are sure they are working for the good of humanity and who feel derouted and frustrated by the unexpected reaction of those human groups among whom they work, who want neither their goods nor their rationality.

The dichotomy by which they wish to delimit us—that of science versus magic—is a false dichotomy. For our science, like magic, is a 'domesticated' kind of thought. The opposition of traditional strata, of peasant masses, to our scientism is not as irrational as it seems in the eyes of administrators, engineers and experts. For the former feel very clearly what these others do not feel—the ethnocentrism and ideology of the latter, even their camouflaged colonialism or imperialism.

Where is the irrational, if irrational there be? It seems more on the side of the planners than on the side of those who question them. And the 'obstacle' to the planners' projects of development or improvement of the standard of living, of rationalisation of nutrition, of health care, should be for them stimuli to awareness of the ideological roots of applied anthropology rather than a point of departure for, or a critique of, science as it is practised today.

We have already stressed the values and norms of Western practical thought in action in the so-called underdeveloped countries. All that we need add is that applied anthropology as we have defined it—that is, as the science of man's manipulative action—can, conversely, integrate into its analyses these profound conscious or unconscious motivations. This is possible since it studies the laws according to which, when one variable is modified, the other elements of the system are transformed, and also since it considers these conscious or unconscious motivations as variables of a system, and discovers the alterations of practice due to its implicit postulates. Here again, it will be possible to bring to light regularities or laws of correlation.

Since there has been a certain time lapse, the fight against slavery allows us now to put into focus some of these regularities and correlations between the motivations of abolitionists (philanthropists, the religious, humanists, or political liberals) and the process of liberation from servitude that resulted in a greater marginalisation of the black. The fact that today the development of a country is expressed in an intensification of marginalisation of certain sectors of the population and even, as has been shown, that this marginalisation is an effect of development—that it cannot avoid creating an unskilled mass in order to be realised at all—suggests that a link also exists between ideologies of planning and its realisation, even though the latter occurs only according to the norms of scientific reason.

Ideologies are collective representations. But there are others which must be taken into account, for example those which encircle the planner himself like a halo. The same is true for the expert as is true for the doctor in our society. He is placed on a continuum whose two poles Max Weber so well defined, i.e. the charismatic leader and the bureaucrat of the rational era. It should be remembered that, if for Weber the charismatic leader comes before the bureaucrat chronologically, Weber did not deny that he could reappear in the course of history, and especially in 'periods of distress—psychic, physical, economic, ethical, religious or political'.

Just as the malady is, for the individual, one of those periods of crisis that transforms the doctor, that expert in medical science, into an 'exceptional' individual with 'special gifts' relevant to the functioning of his body or his mind, so colonisation and decolonisation constitute for the societies that have been submitted to them, periods of distress—and the expert appears as a 'natural leader' who will have the gift of finding for each situation the appropriate remedy. In the minds of those who call on him, he is not a simple administrator of science, since some experts fail and some succeed; he is a man with a certain secularised charisma.

And all the more so because, exactly like the doctor, he deals with men and not only with things. A bureaucratised, rationalised scientist-doctor would discern the malady by its symptoms, and would seek the causes and fight against them with appropriate remedies, scientifically formulated in specialised laboratories for a particular sort of illness. To a certain extent, medicine is in fact taking this direction. But the medical practitioner knows by experience that the malady is not an entity, that what he has before him is a sick man—and not a man who has a sickness—and he acts in a certain way as a result.

Economic, social, or political development plans are at the beginning intent on changing things, that is to transform means of production, institutions, markets or structures. It is only in the face of difficulties encountered that they take account of plans concerning 'persons' rather than only of things to be modified. And there are two results:

(1) If practical applied anthropology as opposed to the theoretical or experimental variety of which we are thinking were a true science, it would only need to concern itself with things and, in applying its rules, would always obtain the desired results. But if it concerns itself with persons, who react very differently to their situations of existence—like the sick to their sicknesses—practical applied anthropology can only be both an art and science at once. That is why we divide it in two, into an experimental science that seeks out the laws of men's action upon things, and into an art that can be rational.

(2) If practical anthropology is an art, the expert, engineer or planner will or will not have the particular gifts that reveal them-

selves when tested and, consequently, he will be judged both as a charismatic leader and as a scholar.[1] We take the view that these collective representations about planners, whatever they may be, constitute to the same degree one of the variables of the system of men's action upon things, of which science should take account in its analyses of the new *homo faber*. And so we arrive at a first rationalisation of the irrational—to the extent that we consider the ideologies of the 'donor' and the more or less mystical reactions of the 'recipient' as 'irrational'—in integrating the non-logical and the logical elements of action into the same theoretical formulation.

When Gurvitch, several years ago, proposed the dual problem of explanation in science and the existence of the liberty of man, he arrived at a similar conclusion to the one we are supporting here. In fact, it seemed to him that the role of scientific activity consisted essentially in the construction of systems of interaction (and not only in the search for causal laws or functional correlations). He showed that the liberty of man could be integrated into these systems in such a way that liberty remained liberty while being at the same time determined, since each system could select as privileged only one particular form of liberty—for example, that of indifference, or that of moral liberty. Surely, the idea we are supporting becomes clearer by this comparison with Gurvitch.

Theoretical applied anthropology, like all science, builds models —but not models of things social, rather models of men's manipulative action on things social. These models should integrate the totality of facts revealed by that action. From there, the irrational elements that we have stressed (and to which others could be added) become rational through this systematisation, while remaining, in their intimate nature, irrational in terms of what we call reason. The comparison with Gurvitch has seemed the best one to clarify what we are calling rationality and the irrational, because Gurvitch, a sociologist, is, like ourselves, interested in global societies and their cultures.

But at the level of the individual, a comparison with psychoanalysis is possible. The psychoanalyst finds himself confronted with behaviour traits that are apparently irrational—phobias, obsessions, delirium. But in turning them into the 'speech' of the unconscious, and in succeeding in making this bizarre speech into a unity of 'discourse,' without destroying the irrational (the pathological is always considered by him as 'pathological') he rationalizes it by integrating it into a genetic or topological system. We say 'rationalises it' because he finds a 'sense' in it.

We hope that the opposition of classical applied anthropology, that is, practical and applied anthropology as a theoretical science of human action, its laws and limits, appears clearer now. In the first instance, the resistance to change does not come from anthropology but from the milieu on which it acts. Consequently, a whole part of the theory of action is left aside, one which seems of the greatest importance—namely the theory of the motivation of the expert, or the social engineer, of his hidden goals; in other words, the analysis of Western reason or science as an ideological form of the functioning of the human mind.

Secondly, it would consider these resistances as the effects of affectivity, prejudice, superstition, and in a Manichean sense vis-à-vis reality as anti-reason. In brief, the obstacle is no longer an element to be integrated but rather a difficulty to be countered by ruse (Western-style planning) or by force (Soviet-style planning). Conversely, we foresee the integration of this anti-reason into the formation of a descriptive system of the alteration of reality by man the planner, an integration which, by giving a direction to this anti-reason, and in linking it to a whole set of inter-relations, 'rationalises' it.

This is the first meaning of our rationalisation of the irrational. In this first sense—just as with liberty in Gurvitch's work—the irrational remains irrational in nature (that is, in opposition to what we call reason). But we think that our conception of applied anthropology can go even further in this rationalisation of the chaos or defiance presented by the irrational to our plans and projects of development. For it substitutes a pluralist notion of reason for a monolithic one. We do not claim to give an exhaustive inventory, or to propose a definitive typology, but with the aid of several examples, to trace the paths of research:

I. The question has been much discussed whether primitive medicine was scientific and rational or only a form of empirical knowledge. Ackerknecht uses the term 'habits' for these therapeutic processes which seem to postulate the existence of a rudimentary science: 'to call such attitudes "naturalistic" or "rational" seems to inject into the data contents they actually do not have.'[2] But is the question correctly phrased? It seems that in fact it would be necessary here to contrast the rational or scientific not with the empirical, or with traditional habits, but with that which has a 'functional efficacity'.[3]

In fact, we find in this popular medicine a whole series of practices that prove to be efficacious. For example, when a mental illness erupts in an individual, since that individual only exists in terms of the place he occupies in an extended family and by virtue of the network that links its other members to himself, we find that it is the family that is treated. The curing of the individual is achieved by means of the re-equilibration of the domestic group (modern psychiatry is only today arriving at this observation which African priests and shamans made long ago).

Many norms that are clothed in a magical aspect in their manifest content have a latent function of real hygiene. Among the Navaho, the practice of defecating far from habitations and in secret is done under the pretext that excrement can be used by a sorcerer to afflict the person in question. The latent function of this custom has empirical effects, unintentional and unrecognised by those who follow it. It protects these Indians against a whole series of infectious diseases.

There is among primitives a 'prevention' of illnesses which naturally takes on different aspects from our own preventive medicine, but which no less expresses the consciousness that the health of individuals concerns the whole group. Thus, we find for example the proscription of sexual relations during epidemics, or among the Yoruba, inoculation against syphilis practised on Omalu adepts long before Jenner invented vaccination.

In a preceding chapter, we spoke of the functionalist perspective in anthropology. Just now we have recognised the 'functional effects' of certain therapeutic or preventive practices in so-called primitive societies. But we prefer to speak in this connection of a 'logic of things' or of acts, that can be different from the 'logic of ideas', both those anchored in tradition and those that wish to change it. There is, in customs that endure, a 'hidden reason' or what anthropologists call their 'latent function'. The social organism reacts to exogenous perturbations with a set of effective measures as do all biological organisms. We fully realise that organicism is condemned in anthropology and sociology alike. But have we not gone too far in the opposite direction in wishing to see in society only the 'social contract,' the work of reason and of will?

Does not the structuralism of Lévi-Strauss (even though he is a declared adversary of functionalism) show us that the structure of societies cannot take just any form? There are types of alliance that are unthinkable because they are destructive of the very conditions of the social. Forms of kinship obey a 'logic' that has its imperative rules. Do not ask us to be certain whether these imperative rules are the 'scar' of the human mind in its cultural workings (the human mind in any case is not our 'reason'; our reason is itself only one of these cultural works) or whether they are inherent in the very being of the social.

We envisage for the moment only this second aspect, whether it is primary or derived is of little import here. It is necessary to recognise that there is a logic of things independent of the logic of our manipulative reason, and which can be infinitely more valid than the latter.

We have gone beyond functionalism. But we had to pass through it because being the more simple, it smoothed our path. Basically, functionalism is the recognition, in a still-superficial form, of *this new type of reason* that we contrast in this provisional attempt at typology with reason of the Western type—honoured by the old applied anthropology—and which we can only define by the term we have already often used, namely 'the logic of things'.

II. Magic has often been compared with science. Frazer for example defined magic as 'false science', false from the point of view of content (which offends our Western reason) but science from the formal point of view. For, unlike religion, which rests on the concept of miracles, magic is based on the existence of causal laws (it is sufficient to say a certain word, or make a certain gesture, for the cause inevitably to produce its effect—it begins to rain, or Satan appears). Comte, Berthelot and many others, historians of human thought, believed that science emerged progressively from magic by replacing—as a result of experience—supernatural causes with natural ones—astronomy for astrology, chemistry for alchemy, medicine for medical magic. On the other hand, Essertier believes that, as with the King of Nimi, science could not replace magic except by first killing it, because science is reason and magic is superstition.[4]

This conflict is an old one and has been superseded. It is superseded because it was posed in the context of a monolothic notion of reason. It must be re-thought today in the context of our own pluralist notion. Is there not a 'magical reason' that may be reason, while at the same time being opposed to our rational reason? The study of certain of the effects of colonisation and decolonisation seems to suggest that there is. We will content ourselves with two undeniable facts elucidated by contemporary ethnography.

The first is that of the opposition between traditional and evolved societies in Africa. Emergent urbanisation and industrialisation and the progressive implanting of individualist values over collective ones, have led to a considerable increase in psychosis and neurosis in major centres of the newly-independent countries. However, those sections of these countries that have remained traditional are also indirectly affected by the movement toward modernisation. New tensions appear there too, and besides there are no totally harmonious societies anywhere; there are always dysfunctional elements in a system.

But native culture furnishes another preventive solution for mental illnesses in religious or magical ritual. In brief, faced with a conflict situation, one can respond to it either by a development of magic or by a descent into madness. We find ourselves in the presence of a law that has been verified elsewhere than in Africa, everywhere where colonisation has occurred, equally in Oceania and among the Amerindians. A society where social disaggregation is not accompanied by cultural disaggregation responds to its traumatisation by a proliferation of magical practices. A society where the native culture has been similarly defeated responds with a proliferation of mental illness.

The second fact is that of the analysis by contemporary ethnographers of the mechanisms by which sorcery responds to social traumatisation. To be brief, we shall only cite a few. In a traditional society, an illness generally has a magical or religious cause. Contact with whites and new conditions of life have brought an increase—often more apparent than real—in mortality or at least in unknown diseases. This cannot be understood if one remains true to the traditional notion, that is, except by surmising that the number of sorcerers has increased. The development of individualistic values can only justify this conclusion, since the sorcerer is by definition he who puts himself outside the human condition, outside the rules of social life, and is thus the pure individualist.

In many African countries, the sorcerer is thought to be like the European, the one who has special powers analogous to those of the whites—to fly in the air, to kill lions, to make mysterious machines. On the other hand, individualism having developed among women, and given the traditional beliefs about feminine jealousy and hatred of husbands, in a society where women were dominated, such individualism is considered as provocative of death of co-wives, infant mortality, or the death of members of the husbands' lineages. Now not only some women but all women —with the increased mortality rate—will be considered as powerful sorcerers even if seen as acting unconsciously or, as in the Ivory Coast, as pawns of the Devil.

But the number of sorcerers increases to such an extent that (1) sorcery can no longer be seen as a chosen activity, learned through special initiation rituals, private to certain individuals or secret societies. It becomes in a way a normal activity of the vast majority of the population while still being seen as unconscious and psychoanalytically based.

(2) Traditional procedures in the fight against sorcery such as the ordeal, confession, or post-mortem analysis of the viscera can no longer suffice in this situation. At the least, they must be integrated into a broader system of a therapeutic type. Once sorcery occurs 'en diable' it must be attacked at its unconscious roots, by the purification of sick souls—from which comes the current proliferation of anti-sorcery aspects of so-called 'prophetic' or messianic movements in Africa.

To a certain extent we find here the 'logic of things' contrasted with the logic of reason. For social organisms defend themselves against such changes as may destroy them, just as during calmer times they defended themselves against internal tensions and dysfunctional elements with a set of compensatory institutions such as rituals of rebellion or magical rites. But this logic of things can no longer maintain the static character we assigned it above, by making it the very condition of existence of the social being as such.

To the extent that societies are transformed by the manipulative action of men, a new logic will appear that takes its start from the former, but makes it dynamic. Rituals to compensate the trauma of change will be retained, but modified to respond to ever new conditions. These modifications do not occur at random; they follow certain rules, like those we enumerated in connection with the growth of sorcery and the multiplication of anti-sorcery movements. As a result, they follow their own logic, that of magical thought.

This logic, while being very different from our own, is equally valid since it allows the acceptance of traumas and dominance over them. And the proof of its validity is that it occurs both in so-called developed and in underdeveloped societies, though perhaps in a less institutionalised form. May we say, moreover, that it is of a statistical order: somatisation of psychic conflicts, internalisation and secularisation of mechanisms of sorcery such as unconscious aggression or rituals of compensation of the sort invented by today's youth. There is then, in our opinion—for it is possible to show by comparison that these laws are general ones—another type of thought than rational thought, and one which accompanies all social mutation. And may we be allowed, for lack of a better phrase, and without giving it a negative connotation, to call it *magical* thought.

Here, where action that follows the laws of Western reason encounters obstacles and resistances, we then find other laws and 'reasons' in play. We could say, paraphrasing Pascal's famous phrase 'the heart has its reasons which the mind knoweth not' (particularly since the heart for Pascal did not correspond to affectivity but to geometric intuition contrasted with algebraic deduction) that things social have their reasons which the mind knoweth not.

In the manipulation of social and cultural reality, various dynamics of thought conflict, cross each other, seek compromises, and displace each other. The 'reason of things' for example, prevents in opposing it, so-called rational reason from destroying life and its organic functions. The conditions of society's existence—in some sense biological and quasi-instinctive—prevent the mechanisation of human relations and the deterioration of ecology. 'Magical' reason does not cause exogenous change to lose its calculated effects, but permits the creation of anti-toxins.

Even if the European judges this reaction to be in his sense pathological, the pathology is in the cause. It is in the change imposed by contact with another civilisation, and with it another form of reason, rather than in the reaction which, on the contrary, is logical and ultimately salutary. Here, the pathological is not in 'things' properly speaking, but in the men who think them.

Applied anthropology should not, if it wishes to become a science, worthy of the name, place reason as it has been formed in Western culture at the centre of its reflection. True, it will have to study the action of men on things, and its effects. But that action—of 'planning' or 'development'—will comprise only one of its chapters. It should encompass all types of action altering and modifying reality and, behind them, all other reasons that our reason does not know at all.

In the first instance, it leads to experimental anthropology—what happens when a given variable is changed—as when money replaces barter, and in various institutions from the market to marriage. In the second instance, it leads to comparative anthropology—comparison of various types of manipulation or of the domestication of reality. In both instances, it elucidates laws—whether these be logical laws or socio-cultural determinisms—that the practitioner will perhaps be able to utilise, but hopefully at least with more prudence, and less ethnocentrism, knowing that man is not a god who can do all, but rather a 'questioner' who should know how to hear the replies made by facts.

NOTES

1. The relationship between the expert and the doctor, which explains the charismatic character of the former, appears especially in curative applied anthropology. What has been called the 'multiple etiology', meaning that the same phenomena can depend on very diverse social or cultural conditions, demands in effect that the expert evaluate and interpret the incidence in each particular case—which implies personal gifts in the utilisation of his scientific knowledge.
2. E. H. Ackerknecht, 'Natural Diseases and Rational Treatment in Primitive Medicine', *Bulletin of the History of Medicine*, XIX, May, 1946, no. 5, pp. 567–97.
3. C. C. Hughes, 'Public Health in Non-Literate Societies', in I. Galdston (ed.), *Man's Image in Medicine and Anthropology*, New York, 1963, pp. 157–233.
4. For a discussion of these various theories, see R. Bastide, *Élements de Sociologie Religieuse*, Colin, Paris, 1935.

Bibliography

Adams, R. N., *Introducción a la Antropologia Aplicada* Seminario de Integracion Social, Guatemala, 1964.

—— 'Notes on the Application of Anthropology' in *Human Organization* 12:2.

Arensberg, C. M., in Polyanyi, K. *et. al.*, *Trade and Markets in Early Empires* The Free Press, Glencoe, 1957.

Balandier, G., 'Le Contexte Socio-Culturel et le Coût Social du Progrès' in *Le Tiers Monde*, Presses Universitaires de France, Paris, 1956.

Barnes, J. A., 'Some Ethical Problems in Modern Fieldwork' in *British Journal of Sociology* 14, 1963.

Barnett, H. G., 'Personal Conflicts and Cultural Change' in *Social Forces*, 20, 1941.

—— *Anthropology in Administration*, Row, Evanston, 1956.

Brameld, T. B. H., *The Remaking of a Culture: Life and Education in Puerto Rico*, Harper, New York, 1959.

—— *Minority Problems in the Public Schools*, Harper, New York, 1946.

Brown, G. and A. Hutt, *Anthropology in Action*, Oxford University Press, London, 1935.

Deutsch, K. N., 'The Price of Integration' in Jacob and Toscans, ed. *The Integration of Political Communities*, Lippincott, Philadelphia, 1964.

Dunn, S. P. & E., 'Soviet Regime and Native Culture in Central Asia and Kazakhstan' in *Current Anthropology*, June, 1967.

Embree, J. F., 'Applied Anthropology and its Relationship to Anthropology' *American Anthropologist* 47, 1945.

Erasmus, C. J., *Man Takes Control*, University of Minnesota Press, Minneapolis, 1961.

Evans-Pritchard, E. E., 'Applied Anthropology' *Africa*, 1946.

Fernandes, F., *Ensaios de Sociologia General e Aplicada*, São Paulo, 1960.

Fisher, G., 'Directed Culture Change in Nayarit, Mexico' in *Synoptic Studies of Culture Change*, New Orleans, 1953.

- Forde, D. ed., *Social Implications of Industrialization and Urbanization in Africa South of the Sahara*, UNESCO, 1956.

Fortes, M., 'Culture Contact as a Dynamic Process' *Africa*, IX, 1, 1936.

Gluckman, M. ed. *Closed System and Open Minds*, Oliver and Boyd, Edinburgh, 1964.

Gurvitch, G., *Traité de Sociologie Tome I* (G. Balandier: Sociologie des régions sous-développeés). *Tome II* (R. Bastide: Problèmes de l'entrecroisement des civilisations et de leurs oeuvres), Presses Universitaires de France, Paris, 1963.

Herskovits, M. J., *Man and His Works*, Alfred Knopf, New York, 1948.

Keesing, F. M., *Culture Change (An Analysis and Bibliography of Anthropological Sources to 1952)*, Stanford University Press, Stanford, 1953.

Kluckhohn, C., *Mirror For Man*, George G. Harrap, London, 1950.

Kroeber, A. L. ed., *Anthropology Today*, Univ. of Chicago Press, Chicago, 1953.

Lebeuf, J. P., *Application de L'Ethnologie à L'Assistance Sanitaire*, Institut de Sociologie Solvay, Brussels, 1957.

Leighton, A. A., ' "Applied" Research and "Pure" Research', *American Anthropologist* 48, 1946.

Linton, R., *The Study of Man*, Appleton-Century Co., New York, 1936.

—— *The Cultural Background of Personality*, D. Appleton-Century Co., New York, 1945.

Loomis, C. P., *Social Systems*, Van Nostrand, Princeton, 1960.

Malinowski, B., 'Practical Anthropology' *Africa*, II, 1, 1929.

Mannheim, K., *Freedom, Power and Democratic Planning*, Int. Lib. of Sociology and Social Reconstruction, New York, 1950.

Mauss, M., 'Divisions et Proportionns de Divisions de la Sociologie' *Année Sociologique* 1927 (chapter 4).

—— 'Appreciation Sociologique du Bolchevisme' *Rev. de Métaphysique et de Morale*, 31, 1924.

Mead, M. ed., *Sociétés, Traditions et Technologie*, UNESCO, 1953.

Métraux, A., *Applied Anthropology in Government*, U.N. Inventory Papers for the Wenner-Gren Foundation, New York 9–20 June, 1952.

Métraux, A. *et al.*, *Resistência à Mudança*, Rio de Janero, 1960.

Nadel, S. F., *Anthropology and Modern Life*, An Inaugural Lecture delivered 10 July, Canberra, 1953.

Parsons, T., *The Structure of Social Action*, The Free Press, Glencoe, 1949.

Redfield, R., *A Village That Chose Progress: Chan Kom Revisited*, Phoenix Books, Chicago, 1948.

—— *The Primitive World and its Transformations*, Cornell University Press, Ithaca, 1953.

Ruopp, P. ed., *Approaches to Community Development*, Mouton & Co., The Hague, 1953.

Sachs, I., *La Découverte du Tiers Monde*, Flammarion, Paris, 1971.

Southall, A. ed., *Social Change in Modern Africa*, International African Seminar I, Makerere, 1954.

Spindler, G. ed., *Education and Anthropology*, Stanford University Press, Stanford, 1955.

Stalin, J., *Marxism and the National and Colonial Question*, Lawrence and Wishart, London, 1942.

Steward, J. H., *Area Research: Theory and Practice*, Social Science Research Council Bulletin 63, 1950.

Tax, S., 'Anthropology and Administration' *Amer. Indigena* 5, 1945.

Ward, B. *et al.*, *Colombia Conference on International Economic Development*, Williamsburg and New York, 1970.

Wirth, L., *Community Life and Social Policy*, Chicago University Press, Chicago, 1956.

Wilson, J. & M., *The Analysis of Social Change*, Cambridge University Press, Cambridge, 1954.

Name Index

Ackerknecht, E. H., 213, 220 n.
Adams, R. N., 71 n., 144, 151 n., 186, 191 n.
Adorno, 195
Allier, R., 12, 25 n.
Allport, G. W., 206 n.
Axlène, A., 197, 206 n.

Bacon, Sir F., 153
Balandier, G., 40, 53, 96, 103 n.
Barnett, H. G., 43, 53, 55 n., 99, 100, 104 n.
Barrès, M., 96
Beauvoir, S. de, 113
Beltram, G. A., 54 n., 55 n., 71 n.
Benedict, R., 143
Benne, K. D., 136 n.
Bennis, W. G., 136 n.
Bentham, J., 27
Bergson, H., 118
Bernard, C., 171
Bernard, J., 183, 206 n.
Berque, J., 5, 9 n., 55 n., 116, 118, 120 n.
Berthelot, 215
Boas, F., 14, 44, 55 n.
Brameld, T., 147, 151 n., 152 n., 197

Cardoso, F. H., 120 n.
Cardoso de Oliveira, R., 151 n.
Caso, A., 71 n.
Chan Kom, 63 ff.
Cherns, A. B., 191 n.
Chin, R., 136 n.
Collins, 197
Comte, A., 1–4, 12, 18, 29, 153, 165, 185, 215

Condominas, 71 n.
Cook, 197
Cooper, 197
Cournot, A. A., 2, 3, 5, 9 n., 207

Descartes, 1–2
Deutsch, 197
Devereux, 50
Dewey, J., 191 n.
Dhoquois, G., 131, 136 n.
Dinerman, 197
Dollard, J., 151 n., 199
Dos Santos, T., 120 n.
Dufrenne, M., 7, 9 n.
Dunn, S. P., 86 n.
Durkheim, E., 4, 6, 9 n., 20, 29, 44, 55 n., 56, 173
Duvignaud, J., 189, 191 n.

Eaton, J. W., 44, 55 n.
Eisenstadt, N. S., 119 n.
Embree, J. F., 30, 32, 36 n.
Engels, F., 165
Essertier, 215

Faidherbe, 58
Fernandes, F., 175, 190 n., 205
Feuerbach, 160, 161
Fisher, G., 71 n.
Fisk, E. K., 106, 119 n.
Fortes, M., 38, 45, 54 n., 55 n.
Fourier, 185
Frank, A. G., 86 n., 120 n.
Frazer, Sir J., 215
Freud, S., 143
Freyer, H., 173, 190 n.